Please renew/return items by last date shown. Please call the number below:

Renewals and enquiries: 0300 1234049

Textphone for hearing or
speech impaired users: 01992 555506

www.hertfordshire.gov.uk/libraries
L32

Also available from BBC Worldwide:

The Nation's Favourite Poems
ISBN: 0 563 38782 3
ISBN: 0 563 38487 5 (hardback gift edition)

The Nation's Favourite Love Poems
ISBN: 0 563 38378 X
ISBN: 0 563 38432 8 (hardback gift edition)

The Nation's Favourite Comic Poems
ISBN: 0 563 38451 4

The Nation's Favourite Twentieth Century Poems
ISBN: 0 563 55143 7

The Nation's Favourite Shakespeare
ISBN: 0 563 55142 9

The Nation's Favourite Poems of Childhood
ISBN: 0 563 55184 4

Audio cassettes available from BBC Radio Collection

The Nation's Favourite Poems
ISBN: 0 563 38987 7

The Nation's Favourite Love Poems
ISBN: 0 563 38279 1

The Nation's Favourite Comic Poems
ISBN: 0 563 55850 4

The Nation's Favourite Shakespeare
ISBN: 0 563 55331 6

The Nation's Favourite Lakeland Poems
ISBN: 0 563 55293 X

The Nation's Favourite Poems of Childhood
ISBN: 0 563 47727 X

The Nation's Favourite Poems of Journeys
ISBN: 0 563 53715 9

The above titles are also available on CD

THE NATION'S
FAVOURITE
ANIMAL POEMS

— ◇ —

FOREWORD BY
VIRGINIA McKENNA

Published by
BBC Worldwide Limited,
Woodlands,
80 Wood Lane,
London
W12 0TT

First published 2001
Edited and compiled by Alex Warwick
Compilation © BBC Worldwide 2001
Poems © individual copyright holders

ISBN: 0 563 53780 9

Set in Stempel Garamond by Keystroke,
Jacaranda Lodge, Wolverhampton.
Printed and bound in Great Britain by Martins the Printers Ltd,
Berwick-upon-Tweed.
Cover printed by Belmont Press, Northampton.

CONTENTS

— ◇ —

– Contents –

'Was it perversity, that I longed to talk to him?
Was it humility, to feel so honoured?
I felt so honoured.'

'There is no sophistry in my body:
My manners are tearing off heads–'

– Contents –

'All things innocent, hapless, forsaken.'

'there trembled through
His happy goodnight air
Some blessed Hope, whereof he knew
And I was unaware.'

'This Chanticleer stood high upon his toes,
He stretched his neck, his eyes began to close,
His beak to open;'

– Contents –

*'Not all that tempts your wandering eyes
And heedless hearts, is lawful prize;
Nor all that glisters, gold.'*

*'Little Lamb, who made thee?
Dost thou know who made thee?'*

FOREWORD BY
VIRGINIA McKENNA

— ◇ —

I have always loved and needed poetry – reading it, scribbling it, thinking it. Poems, good or bad – mostly indifferent – spring to my mind whenever a place, a person or an experience touches an emotional chord. Poetry seems the only way to express my feelings.

So it was with pleasure and excitement that I read this collection of poems about animals that brought together so perfectly two of my greatest interests. And, imagine *my* joy when on the very first page I read:

> what a joy to know,
> even when we can't see or hear you,
> that you are around

W. H. Auden, in his 'Address to the Beasts', sums up for me, in three short lines, the perfect human attitude towards the world's other creatures.

In our must see-it-all, must touch-it-all, must experience-it-all society, just to know something is there and feel happy about it is almost unthinkable. But Auden has rung a clear, sweet starter's bell for this book, and the majority of works echo that refrain. The creatures are praised, admired, feared, smiled on or loved for themselves.

Darker moments momentarily cast their shadows, as in Earle Birney's 'The Bear on the Delhi Road' and Ted Hughes' 'An Otter' – the sad, dancing bear dreaming of fruits in the wilderness, and the hunted otter ending up as a covering tossed onto a chair. But the character and atmosphere of the collection are by no means dark. The 'older' poets are well represented with Wordsworth, Shakespeare, Edgar Allen Poe, Keats and Shelley stirring us with their powerful, rich imagery. I remember, as a schoolgirl, becoming almost overwhelmed by Keats' 'Ode to a Nightingale', and everafter, when I had the good fortune to hear that birdsong, some of the words came tumbling back into my mind.

Sometimes, however, a very direct, unembellished use of language can strike a chord to amuse you or pierce your heart. William Blake's

'The Fly', Norman Maccaig's 'Toad', Ted Hughes' 'Hawk Roosting', Robert Frost's 'Design'... I read them many times and on each occasion increasingly admired the economic approach that achieved such clarity and conveyed such depth of perception. In a way, as I grow older, I am more and more attracted by 'less is more'. That doesn't mean this technique is easy to master when you are trying to express something, but I have often given myself the challenge of seeing how little I need do or say or write to achieve the desired result. Many of these poets *are* masters of this art and if you read the poems aloud you become even more aware of their skill.

Humorous verse and narrative verse are liberally sprinkled throughout the book. Who can fail to remember 'The Owl and the Pussycat' or T. S. Eliot's 'Macavity: the Mystery Cat' – but who, like me, had never read Hilaire Belloc's 'The Vulture' or Edward Lear's 'An Animal Alphabet'?

As for narrative – I have to admit this is one of my favourite forms of poetry. And so, happily for me, two of my special favourites are included here: 'The Snake' by D. H. Lawrence and 'The Fish' by Elizabeth Bishop. Both are deep, strong, stirring poems that have never failed to move me – particularly when I have heard them spoken.

So many extraordinary and gifted men and women share with us, in this volume, their visions, views, wit and remorse, delighting and touching those of us already interested in the animal kingdom and, perhaps – and hopefully – awakening an interest in those whose steps have followed a different path. There is a dazzling variety to entice you – from Sylvia Plath's brilliant 'The Arrival of the Bee Box' to Blake's 'The Tyger'. And you will be able to touch and see and feel to your heart's content.

Virginia McKenna is a founder trustee of the Born Free Foundation.
http://www.bornfree.org.uk

'Between the streams and the red clouds, hearing curlews,
Hearing the horizons endure.'

from 'The Horses'

W. H. AUDEN (1907–73)

ADDRESS TO THE BEASTS

For us who, from the moment
we first are worlded,
lapse into disarray,

who seldom know exactly
what we are up to,
and, as a rule, don't want to,

what a joy to know,
even when we can't see or hear you,
that you are around,

though very few of you
find us worth looking at,
unless we come too close.

To you all scents are sacred
except our smell and those
we manufacture.

How promptly and ably
you execute Nature's policies,
and are never

lured into misconduct
except by some unlucky
chance imprinting.

Endowed from birth with good manners,
you wag no snobbish elbows,
don't leer,

don't look down your nostrils,
nor poke them into another
creature's business.

Your own habitations
are cosy and private, not
pretentious temples.

Of course, you have to take lives
to keep your own, but never
kill for applause.

Compared with even your greediest,
how Non-U
our hunting gentry seem.

Exempt from taxation,
you have never felt the need
to become literate,

but your oral cultures
have inspired our poets to pen
dulcet verses,

and, though unconscious of God,
your Sung Eucharists are
more hallowed than ours.

Instinct is commonly said
to rule you: I would call it
Common Sense.

If you cannot engender
a genius like Mozart,
neither can you

plague the earth
with brilliant sillies like Hegel
or clever nasties like Hobbes.

Shall we ever become adulted,
as you all soon do?
It seems unlikely.

Indeed, one balmy day,
we might well become,
not fossils, but vapour.

Distinct now,
in the end we shall join you
(how soon all corpses look alike),

but you exhibit no signs
of knowing that you are sentenced.
Now, could that be why

we upstarts are often
jealous of your innocence,
but never envious?

EDWIN MUIR (1887–1959)

THE HORSES

Barely a twelvemonth after
The seven days' war that put the world to sleep,
Late in the evening the strange horses came.
By then we had made our convenant with silence,
But in the first few days it was so still
We listened to our breathing and were afraid.
On the second day
The radios failed; we turned the knobs; no answer.
On the third day a warship passed us, heading north,
Dead bodies piled on the deck. On the sixth day
A plane plunged over us into the sea. Thereafter
Nothing. The radios dumb;
And still they stand in corners of our kitchens,
And stand, perhaps, turned on, in a million rooms
All over the world. But now if they should speak,
If on a sudden they should speak again,
If on the stroke of noon a voice should speak,
We would not listen, we would not let it bring
That old bad world that swallowed its children quick
At one great gulp. We would not have it again.
Sometimes we think of the nations lying asleep,
Curled blindly in impenetrable sorrow,
And then the thought confounds us with its strangeness.
The tractors lie about our fields; at evening
They look like dank sea-monsters couched and waiting.
We leave them where they are and let them rust:
'They'll moulder away and be like other loam'.
We make our oxen drag our rusty ploughs,
Long laid aside. We have gone back
Far past our fathers' land.

                                  And then, that evening
Late in the summer the strange horses came.
We heard a distant tapping on the road,
A deepening drumming; it stopped, went on again

And at the corner changed to hollow thunder.
We saw the heads
Like a wild wave charging and were afraid.
We had sold our horses in our fathers' time
To buy new tractors. Now they were strange to us
As fabulous steeds set on an ancient shield
Or illustrations in a book of knights.
We did not dare go near them. Yet they waited,
Stubborn and shy, as if they had been sent
By an old command to find our whereabouts
And that long-lost archaic companionship.
In the first moment we had never a thought
That they were creatures to be owned and used.
Among them were some half-a-dozen colts
Dropped in some wilderness of the broken world,
Yet new as if they had come from their own Eden.
Since then they have pulled our ploughs and borne our loads,
But that free servitude still can pierce our hearts.
Our life is changed; their coming our beginning.

R. S. THOMAS (1913–2000)

THE ANCIENTS OF THE WORLD

The salmon lying in the depths of Llyn Llifon,
  Secretly as a thought in a dark mind,
Is not so old as the owl of Cwm Cowlyd
  Who tells her sorrow nightly on the wind.

The ousel singing in the woods of Cilgwri,
  Tirelessly as a stream over the mossed stones,
Is not so old as the toad of Cors Fochno
  Who feels the cold skin sagging round his bones.

The toad and the ousel and the stag of Rhedynfre,
  That has cropped each leaf from the tree of life,
Are not so old as the owl of Cwm Cowlyd,
  That the proud eagle would have to wife.

MARIANNE MOORE (1887–1972)

ELEPHANTS

Uplifted and waved till immobilized
wistaria-like, the opposing opposed
mouse-gray twined proboscises' trunk formed by two
trunks, fights itself to a spiraled inter-nosed

deadlock of dyke-enforced massiveness. It's a
knock-down drag-out fight that asks no quarter? Just
a pastime, as when the trunk rains on itself
the pool it siphoned up; or when—since each must

provide his forty-pound bough dinner—he broke
the leafy branches. These templars of the Tooth,
these matched intensities, take master care of
master tools. One, sleeping with the calm of youth,

at full length in the half-dry sun-flecked stream-bed,
rests his hunting-horn-curled trunk on shallowed stone.
The sloping hollow of the sleeper's body
cradles the gently breathing eminence's prone

mahout, asleep like a lifeless six-foot
frog, so feather light the elephant's stiff
ear's unconscious of the crossed feet's weight. And the
defenseless human thing sleeps as sound as if

incised with hard wrinkles, embossed with wide ears,
invincibly tusked, made safe by magic hairs!
As if, as if, it is all ifs; we are at
much unease. But magic's masterpiece is theirs—

Houdini's serenity quelling his fears.
Elephant-ear-witnesses-to-be of hymns
and glorias, these ministrants all gray or
gray with white on legs or trunk, are a pilgrims'

pattern of revery not reverence—a
religious procession without any priests,
the centuries-old carefullest unrehearsed
play. Blessed by Buddha's Tooth, the obedient beasts

themselves as toothed temples blessing the street, see
the white elephant carry the cushion that
carries the casket that carries the Tooth.
Amenable to what, matched with him, are gnat

trustees, he does not step on them as the white-
canopied blue-cushioned Tooth is augustly
and slowly returned to the shrine. Though white is
the color of worship and of mourning, he

is not here to worship and he is too wise
to mourn – a life prisoner but reconciled.
With trunk tucked up compactly—the elephant's
sign of defeat—he resisted, but is the child

of reason now. His straight trunk seems to say: when
what we hoped for came to nothing, we revived.
As loss could not ever alter Socrates'
tranquillity, equanimity's contrived

by the elephant. With the Socrates of
animals as with Sophocles the Bee, on whose
tombstone a hive was incised, sweetness tinctures
his gravity. His held-up fore-leg for use

as a stair, to be climbed or descended with
the aid of his ear, expounds the brotherhood
of creatures to man the encroacher, by the
small word with the dot, meaning know—the verb bud.

These knowers 'arouse the feeling that they are
allied to man' and can change roles with their trustees.
Hardship makes the soldier; then teachableness
makes him the philosopher—as Socrates,

prudently testing the suspicious thing, knew
the wisest is he who's not sure that he knows.
Who rides on a tiger can never dismount;
asleep on an elephant, that is repose.

T. S. ELIOT (1888–1965)

THE HIPPOPOTAMUS

Similiter et omnes revereantur Diaconos, ut mandatum Jesu Christi; et
Episcopum, ut Jesum Christum, existentem filius Patris; Presbyteros
autem, ut concilium Dei et conjunctionem Apostolorum. Sine his
Ecclesia non vocatur; de quibus suadeo vos sic habeo.
   S. Ignatii Ad Trallianos
And when this epistle is read among you, cause that it be read also in
the church of the Laodiceans.

The broad-backed hippopotamus
Rests on his belly in the mud;
Although he seems so firm to us
He is merely flesh and blood.

Flesh and blood is weak and frail,
Susceptible to nervous shock;
While the True Church can never fail
For it is based upon a rock.

The hippo's feeble steps may err
In compassing material ends,
While the True Church need never stir
To gather in its dividends.

The 'potamus can never reach
The mango on the mango-tree;
But fruits of pomegranate and peach
Refresh the Church from over sea.

At mating time the hippo's voice
Betrays inflexions hoarse and odd,
But every week we hear rejoice
The Church, at being one with God.

The hippopotamus's day
Is passed in sleep; at night he hunts;
God works in a mysterious way—
The Church can sleep and feed at once.

I saw the 'potamus take wing
Ascending from the damp savannas,
And quiring angels round him sing
The praise of God, in loud hosannas.

Blood of the Lamb shall wash him clean
And him shall heavenly arms enfold,
Among the saints he shall be seen
Performing on a harp of gold.

He shall be washed as white as snow,
By all the martyr'd virgins kist,
While the True Church remains below
Wrapt in the old miasmal mist.

G. K. CHESTERTON (1874–1936)

THE DONKEY

When fishes flew and forests walked
　　And figs grew upon thorn,
Some moment when the moon was blood
　　Then surely I was born.

With monstrous head and sickening cry
　　And ears like errant wings,
The devil's walking parody
　　On all four-footed things.

The tattered outlaw of the earth,
　　Of ancient crooked will;
Starve, scourge, deride me: I am dumb,
　　I keep my secret still.

Fools! For I also had my hour;
　　One far fierce hour and sweet:
There was a shout about my ears,
　　And palms before my feet.

DEBORA GREGER (1949–)

THE FROG IN THE SWIMMING POOL

A wet green velvet scums the swimming pool,
furring the cracks. The deep end swims
in a hatful of rain, not enough to float

the bedspring barge, the tug of shopping cart.
Green-wet himself, the bullfrog holds his court,
sounding the summons to a life so low

he's yet to lure a mate. Under the lip
of concrete slab he reigns, a rumble of rock,
a flickering of sticky tongue that's licked

at any morsel winging into view.
How would he love her? Let me count the waves
that scrape the underside of night and then

let go, the depth of love unplumbed, the breadth,
the height of the pool all he needs to know.
How do I love him? Let me add the weight

of one hush to another, the mockingbird
at midnight echoing itself, not him,
one silence torn in two, sewn shut again.

Down to his level in time wings everything.
He calls the night down on his unlovely head,
on the slimy skin that breathes the slimy air —

the skin that's shed and still he is the same,
the first voice in the world, the last each night.
His call has failed to fill the empty house

across the street, the vacant swing that sways
halfheartedly, the slide slid into rust,
the old griefs waiting burial by the new.

THOMAS HARDY (1840–1928)

THE OXEN

Christmas Eve, and twelve of the clock.
   'Now they are all on their knees,'
An elder said as we sat in a flock
   By the embers in hearthside ease.

We pictured the meek mild creatures where
   They dwelt in their strawy pen,
Nor did it occur to one of us there
   To doubt they were kneeling then.

So fair a fancy few would weave
   In these years! Yet, I feel,
If someone said on Christmas Eve,
   'Come; see the oxen kneel

'In the lonely barton by yonder coomb
   Our childhood used to know,'
I should go with him in the gloom,
   Hoping it might be so.

JOHN CLARE (1793–1864)

HARES AT PLAY

The birds are gone to bed the cows are still
And sheep lie panting on each old mole hill
And underneath the willows grey-green bough
Like toil a resting—lies the fallow plough
The timid hares throw daylights fears away
On the lanes road to dust and dance and play
Then dabble in the grain by nought deterred
To lick the dewfall from the barleys beard
Then out they sturt again and round the hill
Like happy thoughts—dance—squat—and loiter still
Till milking maidens in the early morn
Gingle their yokes and start them in the corn
Through well known beaten paths each nimbling hare
Sturts quick as fear—and seeks its hidden lair

GERARD MANLEY HOPKINS (1844–89)

PIED BEAUTY

Glory be to God for dappled things—
   For skies of couple-colour as a brinded cow;
     For rose-moles all in stipple upon trout that swim;
Fresh-firecoal chestnut-falls; finches' wings;
   Landscape plotted and pieced—fold, fallow, and plough;
     And áll trádes, their gear and tackle and trim.

All things counter, original, spare, strange;
   Whatever is fickle, freckled (who knows how?)
     With swift, slow; sweet, sour; adazzle, dim;
He fathers-forth whose beauty is past change:
           Praise him.

W. B. YEATS (1865–1939)

THE WILD SWANS AT COOLE

The trees are in their autumn beauty,
The woodland paths are dry,
Under the October twilight the water
Mirrors a still sky;
Upon the brimming water among the stones
Are nine-and-fifty swans.

The nineteenth autumn has come upon me
Since I first made my count;
I saw, before I had well finished,
All suddenly mount
And scatter wheeling in great broken rings
Upon their clamorous wings.

I have looked upon those brilliant creatures,
And now my heart is sore.
All's changed since I, hearing at twilight,
The first time on this shore,
The bell-beat of their wings above my head,
Trod with a lighter tread.

Unwearied still, lover by lover,
They paddle in the cold
Companionable streams or climb the air;
Their hearts have not grown old;
Passion or conquest, wander where they will,
Attend upon them still.

But now they drift on the still water,
Mysterious, beautiful;
Among what rushes will they build,
By what lake's edge or pool
Delight men's eyes when I awake some day
To find they have flown away?

TED HUGHES (1930–98)

THE HORSES

I climbed through woods in the hour-before-dawn dark.
Evil air, a frost-making stillness,

Not a leaf, not a bird,—
A world cast in frost. I came out above the wood

Where my breath left tortuous statues in the iron light.
But the valleys were draining the darkness

Till the moorline—blackening dregs of the brightening grey—
Halved the sky ahead. And I saw the horses:

Huge in the dense grey—ten together—
Megalith-still. They breathed, making no move,

With draped manes and tilted hind-hooves,
Making no sound.

I passed: not one snorted or jerked its head.
Grey silent fragments

Of a grey silent world.

I listened in emptiness on the moor-ridge.
The curlew's tear turned its edge on the silence.

Slowly detail leafed from the darkness. Then the sun
Orange, red, red erupted.

Silently, and splitting to its core tore and flung cloud,
Shook the gulf open, showed blue,

And the big planets hanging—
I turned

Stumbling in the fever of a dream, down towards
The dark woods, from the kindling tops,

And came to the horses.
                    There, still they stood,
But now steaming and glistening under the flow of light,

Their draped stone manes, their tilted hind-hooves
Stirring under a thaw while all around them

The frost showed its fires. But still they made no sound.
Not one snorted or stamped,

Their hung heads patient as the horizons
High over valleys, in the red levelling rays—

In din of the crowded streets, going among the years, the faces,
May I still meet my memory in so lonely a place

Between the streams and the red clouds, hearing curlews,
Hearing the horizons endure.

*'Oh I am a cat that likes to
Gallop about doing good'*

from 'The Galloping Cat'

AMY CLAMPITT (1920–94)

THE CORMORANT IN ITS ELEMENT

That bony potbellied arrow, wing-pumping along
implacably, with a ramrod's rigid adherence,
airborne, to the horizontal, discloses talents
one would never have guessed at. Plummeting

waterward, big black feet splayed for a landing
gear, slim head turning and turning, vermilion-
strapped, this way and that, with a lightning glance
over the shoulder, the cormorant astounding-

ly, in one sleek involuted arabesque, a vertical
turn on a dime, goes into that inimitable
vanishing-and-emerging-from-under-the-briny-

deep act which, unlike the works of Homo Houdini,
is performed for reasons having nothing at all
to do with ego, guilt, ambition, or even money.

NORMAN MACCAIG (1910–96)

KINGFISHER

That kingfisher jewelling upstream
seems to leave a streak of itself behind it
in the bright air. The trees
are all the better for its passing.

It's not a mineral eater, though it looks it:
It doesn't nip nicks out of the edges
of rainbows. — It dives
into the burly water, then, perched
on a Japanese bough, gulps
into its own incandescence
a wisp of minnow, a warrior stickleback.
— Or it vanishes into its burrow, resplendent
Samurai, returning home
to his stinking slum.

ELIZABETH BISHOP (1911–79)

SANDPIPER

The roaring alongside he takes for granted,
and that every so often the world is bound to shake.
He runs, he runs to the south, finical, awkward,
in a state of controlled panic, a student of Blake.

The beach hisses like fat. On his left, a sheet
of interrupting water comes and goes
and glazes over his dark and brittle feet.
He runs, he runs straight through it, watching his toes.

—Watching, rather, the spaces of sand between them,
where (no detail too small) the Atlantic drains
rapidly backwards and downwards. As he runs,
he stares at the dragging grains.

The world is a mist. And then the world is
minute and vast and clear. The tide
is higher or lower. He couldn't tell you which.
His beak is focused; he is preoccupied,

looking for something, something, something.
Poor bird, he is obsessed!
The millions of grains are black, white, tan, and gray,
mixed with quartz grains, rose and amethyst.

NORMAN MACCAIG (1910–96)

SOLITARY CROW

Why solitary crow? He in his feathers
Is a whole world of crow—of a dry-stick nest,
Of windy distances where to be crow is best,
Of tough-guy clowning and of black things done
To a sprawled lamb whose blood beads in the sun.

Sardonic anarchist. Where he goes he carries,
Since there's no centre, what a centre is,
And that is crow, the ragged self that's his.
Smudged on a cloud, he jeers at the world then halts
To jeer at himself and turns two somersaults.

He ambles through the air, flops down and seesaws
On a blunt fencepost, hiccups and says *Caw*.
The sun glints greasy on his working craw
And adds a silver spot to that round eye
Whose black light bends and cocks the world awry.

OGDEN NASH (1902–71)

THE DUCK

Behold the duck.
It does not cluck.
A cluck it lacks.
It quacks.
It is specially fond
Of a puddle or pond.
When it dines or sups,
It bottoms ups.

EDWARD LEAR (1812–88)

AN ANIMAL ALPHABET

A   The Absolutely Abstemious Ass,
    who resided in a Barrel, and only lived on
    Soda Water and Pickled Cucumbers.

B   The Bountiful Beetle,
    who always carried a Green Umbrella when it didn't rain,
    and left it at home when it did.

C   The Comfortable Confidential Cow,
    who sate in her Red Morocco Armchair and
    toasted her own Bread at the parlour Fire.

D   The Dolomphious Duck,
    who caught spotted frogs for her dinner
    with a Runcible Spoon.

E   The Enthusiastic Elephant,
    who ferried himself across the water with the
    Kitchen Poker and a New pair of Ear-rings.

F   The Fizzgiggious Fish,
    who always walked about upon Stilts,
    because he had no legs.

G   The Good-natured Gray Gull,
    who carried the Old Owl, and his Crimson Carpetbag,
    across the river, because he could not swim.

H   The Hasty Higgeldipiggledy Hen,
    who went to market in a Blue Bonnet and Shawl,
    and bought a Fish for Supper.

I   The Inventive Indian,
    who caught a Remarkable Rabbit in a
    Stupendous Silver Spoon.

J   The Judicious Jubilant Jay,
    who did up her Back Hair every morning with a Wreath of Roses,
    Three feathers, and a Gold Pin.

K   The Kicking Kangaroo,
    who wore a Pale Pink Muslin dress
    with Blue spots.

L   The Lively Learned Lobster,
    who mended his own Clothes with
    a Needle and Thread.

M   The Melodious Meritorious Mouse,
    who played a merry minuet on the
    Pianoforte.

N   The Nutritious Newt,
    who purchased a Round Plum-pudding,
    for his granddaughter.

O   The Obsequious Ornamental Ostrich,
    who wore boots to keep his
    feet quite dry.

P   The Perpendicular Purple Polly,
    who read the Newspaper and ate Parsnip Pie
    with his Spectacles.

Q   The Queer Querulous Quail,
    who smoked a pipe of tobacco on the top of
    a Tin Tea-kettle.

R   The Rural Runcible Raven,
    who wore a White Wig and flew away
    with the Carpet Broom.

S   The Scroobious Snake,
who always wore a Hat on his Head, for
fear he should bite anybody.

T   The Tumultuous Tom-tommy Tortoise,
who beat a Drum all day long in the
middle of the wilderness.

U   The Umbrageous Umbrella-maker,
whose Face nobody ever saw, because it was
always covered by his Umbrella.

V   The Visibly Vicious Vulture,
who wrote some verses to a Veal-cutlet in a
Volume bound in Vellum.

W   The Worrying Whizzing Wasp,
who stood on a Table, and played sweetly on a
Flute with a Morning Cap.

X   The Excellent Double-extra XX
imbibing King Xerxes, who lived a
long while ago.

Y   The Yonghy-Bonghy-Bo,
whose Head was ever so much bigger than his
Body, and whose Hat was rather small.

Z   The Zigzag Zealous Zebra,
who carried five Monkeys on his back all
the way to Jellibolee.

JOHN BUNYAN (1628–88)

UPON A SNAIL

She goes but softly, but she goeth sure,
　　She stumbles not, as stronger creatures do;
Her journey's shorter, so she may endure
　　Better than they which do much further go.

She makes no noise, but stilly seizeth on
　　The flower or herb appointed for her food;
The which she quietly doth feed upon,
　　While others range, and glare, but find no good.

And though she doth but very softly go,
　　However slow her pace be, yet 'tis sure;
And certainly they that do travel so,
　　The prize which they do aim at, they procure.

THOM GUNN (1929–)

CONSIDERING THE SNAIL

The snail pushes through a green
night, for the grass is heavy
with water and meets over
the bright path he makes, where rain
has darkened the earth's dark. He
moves in a wood of desire,

pale antlers barely stirring
as he hunts. I cannot tell
what power is at work, drenched there
with purpose, knowing nothing.
What is a snail's fury? All
I think is that if later

I parted the blades above
the tunnel and saw the thin
trail of broken white across
litter, I would never have
imagined the slow passion
to that deliberate progress.

THOM GUNN (1929–)

APARTMENT CATS

The Girls wake, stretch, and pad up to the door.
    They rub my leg and purr:
      One sniffs around my shoe,
      Rich with an outside smell,
    The other rolls back on the floor —
White bib exposed, and stomach of soft fur.

Now, more awake, they re-enact Ben Hur
    Along the corridor,
      Wheel, gallop; as they do,
      Their noses twitching still,
    Their eyes get wild, their bodies tense,
Their usual prudence seemingly withdraws.

And then they wrestle: parry, lock of paws,
    Blind hug of close defence,
      Tail-thump, and smothered mew.
      If either, though, feels claws,
    She abruptly rises, knowing well
How to stalk off in wise indifference.

STEVIE SMITH (1902–71)

THE GALLOPING CAT

Oh I am a cat that likes to
Gallop about doing good
So
One day when I was
Galloping about doing good, I saw
A Figure in the path; I said:
Get off! (Be-
cause
I am a cat that likes to
Gallop about doing good)
But he did not move, instead
He raised his hand as if
To land me a cuff
So I made to dodge so as to
Prevent him bring it orf,
Un-for-tune-ately I slid
On a banana skin
Some Ass had left instead
Of putting in the bin. So
His hand caught me on the cheek
I tried
To lay his arm open from wrist to elbow
With my sharp teeth
Because I am
A cat that likes to gallop about doing good.
Would you believe it?
He wasn't there
My teeth met nothing but air,
But a Voice said: Poor cat,
(Meaning me) and a soft stroke
Came on me head
Since when
I have been bald.
I regard myself as

A martyr to doing good.
Also I heard a swoosh
As of wings, and saw
A halo shining at the height of
Mrs Gubbins's backyard fence,
So I thought: What's the good
Of galloping about doing good
When angels stand in the path
And do not do as they should
Such as having an arm to be bitten off
All the same I
Intend to go on being
A cat that likes to
Gallop about doing good
So
Now with my bald head I go,
Chopping the untidy flowers down, to and fro,
An' scooping up the grass to show
Underneath
The cinder path of wrath
Ha ha ha ha, ho,
Angels aren't the only ones who do not know
What's what and that
Galloping about doing good
Is a full-time job
That needs
An experienced eye of earthly
Sharpness, worth I dare say
(If you'll forgive a personal note)
A good deal more
Than all that skyey stuff
Of angels that make so bold as
To pity a cat like me that
Gallops about doing good.

PAUL MULDOON (1951–)

BROCK

Small wonder
he's not been sighted all winter;
this old brock's
been to Normandy and back

through the tunnels and trenches
of his subconscious.
His father fell victim
to mustard-gas at the Somme;

one of his sons lost a paw
to a gin-trap at Lisbellaw:
another drills
on the Antrim hills'

still-molten lava
in a moth-eaten Balaclava.
An elaborate
system of foxholes and duckboards

leads to the terminal moraine
of an ex-linen baron's
croquet-lawn
where he's part-time groundsman.

I would find it somewhat *infra dig*
to dismiss him simply as a pig
or heed Gerald of Wales'
tall tales

of badgers keeping badger-slaves.
For when he shuffles
across the esker
I glimpse my grandfather's whiskers

stained with tobacco-pollen.
When he piddles against a bullaun
I know he carries bovine TB
but what I *see*

is my father in his Sunday suit's
bespoke lime and lignite
patrolling his now-diminished estate
and taking stock of this and that.

SUZANNE KNOWLES (1911–)

FOX DANCING

Tall as a foxglove spire, on tiptoe
The fox in the wilderness dances;
His pelt and burnished claws reflect
The sun's and the moon's glances.

From blackberry nose to pride of tail
He is elegant, he is gay;
With his pawsteps as a pattern of joy
He transfigures the day.

For a hat he wears a rhubarb leaf
To keep his thinking cool,
Through which his fur-lined ears prick up.
This fox, he is no fool

And does not give a good-morning
For the condition of his soul:
With the fox dancing in the desert
Study to be whole.

'Was it perversity, that I longed to talk to him?
Was it humility, to feel so honoured?
I felt so honoured.'

from 'Snake'

JOHN DONNE (1572–1631)

THE FLEA

Mark but this flea, and mark in this,
How little that which thou deny'st me is;
It suck'd me first, and now sucks thee,
And in this flea, our two bloods mingled be;
Thou know'st that this cannot be said
A sin, nor shame, nor loss of maidenhead,
    Yet this enjoys before it woo,
      And pamper'd swells with one blood made of two,
      And this, alas, is more than we would do.

Oh stay, three lives in one flea spare,
Where we almost, yea more than married are.
This flea is you and I, and this
Our marriage bed, and marriage temple is;
Though parents grudge, and you, we're met,
And cloister'd in these living walls of jet.
    Though use make you apt to kill me,
      Let not to that, self-murder added be,
      And sacrilege, three sins in killing three.

Cruel and sudden, hast thou since
Purpled thy nail, in blood of innocence?
Wherein could this flea guilty be,
Except in that drop which it suck'd from thee?
Yet thou triumph'st, and say'st that thou
Find'st not thyself, nor me, the weaker now;
    'Tis true, then learn how false, fears be;
      Just so much honor, when thou yield'st to me,
      Will waste, as this flea's death took life from thee.

D. H. LAWRENCE (1885–1930)

MOSQUITO

When did you start your tricks
Monsieur?

What do you stand on such high legs for?
Why this length of shredded shank
You exaltation?

Is it so that you shall lift your centre of gravity upwards
And weigh no more than air as you alight upon me,
Stand upon me weightless, you phantom?

I heard a woman call you the Winged Victory
In sluggish Venice.
You turn your head towards your tail, and smile.

How can you put so much devilry
Into that translucent phantom shred
Of a frail corpus?

Queer, with your thin wings and your streaming legs
How you sail like a heron, on a dull clot of air,
A nothingness.

Yet what an aura surrounds you;
Your evil little aura, prowling, and casting a numbness on my mind.

That is your trick, your bit of filthy magic:
Invisibility, and the anaesthetic power
To deaden my attention in your direction.

But I know your game now, streaky sorcerer.

Queer, how you stalk and prowl the air
In circles and evasions, enveloping me,
Ghoul on wings
Winged Victory.

Settle, and stand on long thin shanks
Eyeing me sideways, and cunningly conscious that I am aware,
You speck.

I hate the way you lurch off sideways into air
Having read my thoughts against you.

Come then, let us play at unawares,
And see who wins in this sly game of bluff,
Man or mosquito.

You don't know that I exist, and I don't know that you exist.
Now then!

It is your trump
It is your hateful little trump
You pointed fiend,
Which shakes my sudden blood to hatred of you:
It is your small, high, hateful bugle in my ear.

Why do you do it?
Surely it is bad policy.

They say you can't help it.

If that is so, then I believe a little in Providence protecting the innocent.
But it sounds so amazingly like a slogan,
A yell of triumph as you snatch my scalp.

Blood, red blood
Super-magical
Forbidden liquor.

I behold you stand
For a second enspasmed in oblivion,

Obscenely ecstasied
Sucking live blood,
My blood.

Such silence, such suspended transport,
Such gorging,
Such obscenity of trespass.

You stagger
As well as you may.
Only your accursed hairy frailty
Your own imponderable weightlessness
Saves you, wafts you away on the very draught my anger makes in its
    snatching.

Away with a paean of derision
You winged blood-drop.

Can I not overtake you?
Are you one too many for me,
Winged Victory?
Am I not mosquito enough to out-mosquito you?

Queer, what a big stain my sucked blood makes
Beside the infinitesimal faint smear of you!
Queer, what a dim dark smudge you have disappeared into!

JOHN MONTAGUE (1929–)

THE TROUT
For Barrie Cooke

Flat on the bank I parted
Rushes to ease my hands
In the water without a ripple
And tilt them slowly downstream
To where he lay, tendril-light,
In his fluid sensual dream.

Bodiless lord of creation
I hung briefly above him
Savouring my own absence,
Senses expanding in the slow
Motion, the photographic calm
That grows before action.

As the curve of my hands
Swung under his body
He surged, with visible pleasure.
I was so preternaturally close
I could count every stipple
But still cast no shadow, until

The two palms crossed in a cage
Under the lightly pulsing gills.
Then (entering my own enlarged
Shape, which rode on the water)
I gripped. To this day I can
Taste his terror on my hands.

ELIZABETH BISHOP (1911–79)

THE FISH

I caught a tremendous fish
and held him beside the boat
half out of water, with my hook
fast in a corner of his mouth.
He didn't fight.
He hadn't fought at all.
He hung a grunting weight,
battered and venerable
and homely. Here and there
his brown skin hung in strips
like ancient wallpaper,
and its pattern of darker brown
was like wallpaper:
shapes like full-blown roses
stained and lost through age.
He was speckled with barnacles,
fine rosettes of lime,
and infested
with tiny white sea-lice,
and underneath two or three
rags of green weed hung down.
While his gills were breathing in
the terrible oxygen
—the frightening gills,
fresh and crisp with blood,
that can cut so badly—
I thought of the coarse white flesh
packed in like feathers,
the big bones and the little bones,
the dramatic reds and blacks
of his shiny entrails,
and the pink swim-bladder
like a big peony.
I looked into his eyes

which were far larger than mine
but shallower, and yellowed,
the irises backed and packed
with tarnished tinfoil
seen through the lenses
of old scratched isinglass.
They shifted a little, but not
to return my stare.
—It was more like the tipping
of an object toward the light.
I admired his sullen face,
the mechanism of his jaw,
and then I saw
that from his lower lip
—if you could call it a lip—
grim, wet, and weaponlike,
hung five old pieces of fish-line,
or four and a wire leader
with the swivel still attached,
with all their five big hooks
grown firmly in his mouth.
A green line, frayed at the end
where he broke it, two heavier lines,
and a fine black thread
still crimped from the strain and snap
when it broke and he got away.
Like medals with their ribbons
frayed and wavering,
a five-haired beard of wisdom
trailing from his aching jaw.
I stared and stared
and victory filled up
the little rented boat,
from the pool of bilge

where oil had spread a rainbow
around the rusted engine
to the bailer rusted orange,
the sun-cracked thwarts,
the oarlocks on their strings,
the gunnels—until everything
was rainbow, rainbow, rainbow!
And I let the fish go.

ROBERT BURNS (1759–96)

TO A MOUSE
On Turning Her up in Her Nest with the Plough, November, 1785

Wee, sleekit, cow'rin, tim'rous beastie,
O, what a panic's in thy breastie!
Thou need na start awa sae hasty,
          Wi' bickering brattle!
I wad be laith to rin an' chase thee,
          Wi' murd'ring pattle!

I'm truly sorry man's dominion
Has broken Nature's social union,
An' justifies that ill opinion
          Which makes thee startle
At me, thy poor earth-born companion,
          An' fellow-mortal!

I doubt na, whiles, but thou may thieve;
What then? poor beastie, thou maun live!
A daimen icker in a thrave
          'S a sma' request:
I'll get a blessin wi' the lave,
          And never miss't!

Thy wee bit housie, too, in ruin!
Its silly wa's the win's are strewin!
An' naething, now, to big a new ane,
          O' foggage green!
An' bleak December's winds ensuin,
          Baith snell an' keen!

Thou saw the fields laid bare and waste,
An' weary winter comin fast,
An' cozie here, beneath the blast,
          Thou thought to dwell,
Till crash! the cruel coulter past
          Out thro' thy cell.

51

That wee bit heap o' leaves an' stibble
Has cost thee mony a weary nibble!
Now thou's turned out, for a' thy trouble,
      But house or hald,
To thole the winter's sleety dribble,
        An' cranreuch cauld!

But, Mousie, thou art no thy lane,
In proving foresight may be vain:
The best laid schemes o' mice an' men
      Gang aft a-gley.
An' lea'e us nought but grief an' pain
      For promised joy.

Still thou art blest, compared wi' me!
The present only toucheth thee:
But och! I backward cast my e'e
      On prospects drear!
An' forward, tho' I canna see,
      I guess an' fear!

WILLIAM COWPER (1731–1800)

EPITAPH ON A HARE

Here lies, whom hound did ne'er pursue,
    Nor swifter greyhound follow,
Whose foot ne'er tainted morning dew,
    Nor ear heard huntsman's hallo',

Old Tiney, surliest of his kind,
    Who, nursed with tender care,
And to domestic bounds confined,
    Was still a wild jack-hare.

Though duly from my hand he took
    His pittance every night,
He did it with a jealous look,
    And, when he could, would bite.

His diet was of wheaten bread,
    And milk, and oats, and straw,
Thistles, or lettuces instead,
    With sand to scour his maw.

On twigs of hawthorn he regaled,
    On pippins' russet peel;
And, when his juicy salads failed,
    Sliced carrot pleased him well.

A Turkey carpet was his lawn,
    Whereon he loved to bound,
To skip and gambol like a fawn,
    And swing his rump around.

His frisking was at evening hours,
    For then he lost his fear;
But most before approaching showers,
    Or when a storm drew near.

Eight years and five round-rolling moons
    He thus saw steal away,
Dozing out all his idle noons,
    And every night at play.

I kept him for his humor's sake,
    For he would oft beguile
My heart of thoughts that made it ache,
    And force me to a smile.

But now, beneath this walnut-shade
    He finds his long, last home,
And waits in snug concealment laid,
    Till gentler Puss shall come.

He, still more agèd, feels the shocks
    From which no care can save,
And, partner once of Tiney's box,
    Must soon partake his grave.

NORMAN NICHOLSON (1914–)

THE TAME HARE

She came to him in dreams—her ears
Diddering like antennae, and her eyes
Wide as dark flowers where the dew
Holds and dissolves a purple hoard of shadow.
The thunder clouds crouched back, and the world opened
Tiny and bright as a celandine after rain.
A gentle light was on her, so that he
Who saw the talons in the vetch
Remembered now how buttercup and daisy
Would bounce like springs when a child's foot stepped off them.
Oh, but never dared he touch—
Her fur was still electric to the fingers.

Yet of all the beasts blazoned in gilt and blood
In the black-bound scriptures of his mind,
Pentecostal dove and paschal lamb,
Eagle, lion, serpent, she alone
Lived also in the noon of ducks and sparrows;
And the cleft-mouthed kiss which plugged the night with fever
Was sweetened by a lunch of docks and lettuce.

EARLE BIRNEY (1904–91)

THE BEAR ON THE DELHI ROAD

Unreal   tall as a myth
by the road the Himalayan bear
is beating the brilliant air
with his crooked arms
About him two men   bare
spindly as locusts   leap
One pulls on a ring
in the great soft nose   His mate
flicks   flicks with a stick
up at the rolling eyes

They have not led him here
down from the fabulous hills
to this bald alien plain
and the clamorous world   to kill
but simply to teach him to dance

They are peaceful both   these spare
men of Kashmir   and the bear
alive is their living   too
If   far on the Delhi way
around him galvanic they dance
it is merely to wear   wear
from his shaggy body the tranced
wish forever to stay
only an ambling bear
four-footed in berries

It is no more joyous for them
in this hot dust to prance
out of reach of the praying claws
sharpened to paw for ants
in the shadows of deodars
It is not easy to free

myth from reality
or rear this fellow up
to lurch   lurch with them
in the tranced dancing of men

SYLVIA PLATH (1932–63)

THE ARRIVAL OF THE BEE BOX

I ordered this, this clean wood box
Square as a chair and almost too heavy to lift.
I would say it was the coffin of a midget
Or a square baby
Were there not such a din in it.

The box is locked, it is dangerous.
I have to live with it overnight
And I can't keep away from it.
There are no windows, so I can't see what is in there.
There is only a little grid, no exit.

I put my eye to the grid.
It is dark, dark,
With the swarmy feeling of African hands
Minute and shrunk for export,
Black and black, angrily clambering.

How can I let them out?
It is the noise that appals me most of all,
The unintelligible syllables.
It is like a Roman mob,
Small, taken one by one, but my god, together!

I lay my ear to furious Latin.
I am not a Caesar.
I have simply ordered a box of maniacs.
They can be sent back.
They can die, I need feed them nothing, I am the owner.

I wonder how hungry they are.
I wonder if they would forget me
If I just undid the locks and stood back and turned into a tree.
There is the laburnum, its blond colonnades,
And the petticoats of the cherry.

They might ignore me immediately
In my moon suit and funeral veil.
I am no source of honey
So why should they turn on me?
Tomorrow I will be sweet God, I will set them free.

The box is only temporary.

EMILY DICKINSON (1830–86)

'A NARROW FELLOW IN THE GRASS'

A narrow Fellow in the Grass
Occasionally rides—
You may have met Him—did you not
His notice sudden is—

The Grass divides as with a Comb—
A spotted shaft is seen—
And then it closes at your feet
And opens further on—

He likes a Boggy Acre
A Floor too cool for Corn—
Yet when a Boy, and Barefoot—
I more than once at Noon
Have passed, I thought, a Whip lash
Unbraiding in the Sun
When stooping to secure it
It wrinkled, and was gone—

Several of Nature's people
I know, and they know me—
I feel for them a transport
Of cordiality—

But never met this Fellow
Attended, or alone
Without a tighter breathing
And Zero at the Bone—

A. K. RAMANUJAN (1929–93)

SNAKES

No, it does not happen
when I walk through the woods.
But, walking in museums of quartz
or the aisles of bookstacks,
looking at their geometry
without curves
and the layers of transparency
that make them opaque,
dwelling on the yellower vein
in the yellow amber
or touching a book that has gold
on its spine,
        I think of snakes.

The twirls of their hisses
rise like the tiny dust-cones on slow-noon roads
winding through the farmers' feet.
Black lorgnettes are etched on their hoods,
ridiculous, alien, like some terrible aunt,
a crest among tiles and scales
that moult with the darkening half
of every moon.

A basketful of ritual cobras
comes into the tame little house,
their brown-wheat glisten ringed with ripples.
They lick the room with their bodies, curves
uncurling, writing a sibilant alphabet of panic
on my floor. Mother gives them milk
in saucers. She watches them suck
and bare the black-line design
etched on the brass of the saucer.
The snakeman wreathes their writhing
round his neck

for father's smiling
money. But I scream.

Sister ties her braids
with a knot of tassel.
But the weave of her knee-long braid has scales,
their gleaming held by a score of clean new pins.
I look till I see her hair again.
My night full of ghosts from a sadness
in a play, my left foot listens to my right footfall,
a clockwork clicking in the silence
within my walking.
                    The clickshod heel suddenly strikes
and slushes on a snake: I see him turn,
the green white of his belly
measured by bluish nodes, a water-bleached lotus stalk
plucked by a landsman hand. Yet panic rushes
my body to my feet, my spasms wring
and drain his fear and mine. I leave him sealed,
a flat-head whiteness on a stain.
                                        Now
frogs can hop upon this sausage rope,
flies in the sun will mob the look in his eyes,

and I can walk through the woods.

D. H. LAWRENCE (1885–1930)

SNAKE

A snake came to my water-trough
On a hot, hot day, and I in pyjamas for the heat,
To drink there.

In the deep, strange-scented shade of the great dark carob-tree
I came down the steps with my pitcher
And must wait, must stand and wait, for there he was at the trough
    before me.

He reached down from a fissure in the earth-wall in the gloom
And trailed his yellow-brown slackness soft-bellied down, over the
    edge of the stone trough
And rested his throat upon the stone bottom,
And where the water had dripped from the tap, in a small clearness,
He sipped with his straight mouth,
Softly drank through his straight gums, into his slack long body,
Silently.

Someone was before me at my water-trough,
And I, like a second comer, waiting.

He lifted his head from his drinking, as cattle do,
And looked at me vaguely, as drinking cattle do,
And flickered his two-forked tongue from his lips, and mused a
    moment,
And stooped and drank a little more,
Being earth-brown, earth-golden from the burning bowels of the earth
On the day of Sicilian July, with Etna smoking.
The voice of my education said to me
He must be killed,
For in Sicily the black, black snakes are innocent, the gold are
    venomous.

And voices in me said, If you were a man
You would take a stick and break him now, and finish him off.

But must I confess how I liked him,
How glad I was he had come like a guest in quiet, to drink at my
    water-trough

And depart peaceful, pacified, and thankless,
Into the burning bowels of this earth?

Was it cowardice, that I dared not kill him?
Was it perversity, that I longed to talk to him?
Was it humility, to feel so honoured?
I felt so honoured.
And yet those voices:
If you were not afraid, you would kill him!

And truly I was afraid, I was most afraid,
But even so, honoured still more
That he should seek my hospitality
From out the dark door of the secret earth.

He drank enough
And lifted his head, dreamily, as one who has drunken,
And flickered his tongue like a forked night on the air, so black,
Seeming to lick his lips,
And looked around like a god, unseeing, into the air,
And slowly turned his head,
And slowly, very slowly, as if thrice adream,
Proceeded to draw his slow length curving round
And climb again the broken bank of my wall-face.

And as he put his head into that dreadful hole,
And as he slowly drew up, snake-easing his shoulders, and entered
    farther,
A sort of horror, a sort of protest against his withdrawing into that
    horrid black hole,

Deliberately going into the blackness, and slowly drawing himself
   after,
Overcame me now his back was turned.

I looked round, I put down my pitcher,
I picked up a clumsy log
And threw it at the water-trough with a clatter.

I think it did not hit him,
But suddenly that part of him that was left behind convulsed in
   undignified haste.
Writhed like lightning, and was gone
Into the black hole, the earth-lipped fissure in the wall-front,
At which, in the intense still noon, I stared with fascination.

And immediately I regretted it.
I thought how paltry, how vulgar, what a mean act!
I despised myself and the voices of my accursed human education.

And I thought of the albatross
And I wished he would come back, my snake.

For he seemed to me again like a king,
Like a king in exile, uncrowned in the underworld,
Now due to be crowned again.

And so, I missed my chance with one of the lords
Of life.
And I have something to expiate;
A pettiness.

ROBERT FROST (1874–1963)

COME IN

As I came to the edge of the woods,
Thrush music—hark!
Now if it was dusk outside,
Inside it was dark.

Too dark in the woods for a bird
By sleight of wing
To better its perch for the night,
Though it still could sing.

The last of the light of the sun
That had died in the west
Still lived for one song more
In a thrush's breast.

Far in the pillared dark
Thrush music went—
Almost like a call to come in
To the dark and lament.

But no, I was out for stars;
I would not come in.
I meant not even if asked;
And I hadn't been.

'There is no sophistry in my body:
My manners are tearing off heads—'
from 'Hawk Roosting'

WILLIAM BLAKE (1757–1827)

THE TYGER

Tyger! Tyger! burning bright
In the forests of the night,
What immortal hand or eye
Could frame thy fearful symmetry?

In what distant deeps or skies
Burnt the fire of thine eyes?
On what wings dare he aspire?
What the hand, dare seize the fire?

And what shoulder, & what art,
Could twist the sinews of thy heart?
And when thy heart began to beat,
What dread hand? & what dread feet?

What the hammer? what the chain?
In what furnace was thy brain?
What the anvil? what dread grasp
Dare its deadly terrors clasp?

When the stars threw down their spears,
And water'd heaven with their tears,
Did he smile his work to see?
Did he who made the Lamb make thee?

Tyger! Tyger! burning bright
In the forests of the night,
What immortal hand or eye
Dare frame thy fearful symmetry?

RUDYARD KIPLING (1865–1936)

THE HYAENAS

After the burial-parties leave
    And the baffled kites have fled;
The wise hyaenas come out at eve
    To take account of our dead.

How he died and why he died
    Troubles them not a whit.
They snout the bushes and stones aside
    And dig till they come to it.

They are only resolute they shall eat
    That they and their mates may thrive,
And they know that the dead are safer meat
    Than the weakest thing alive.

(For a goat may butt, and a worm may sting,
    And a child will sometimes stand;
But a poor dead soldier of the King
    Can never lift a hand.)

They whoop and halloo and scatter the dirt
    Until their tushes white
Take good hold in the army shirt,
    And tug the corpse to light,

And the pitiful face is shewn again
    For an instant ere they close;
But it is not discovered to living men—
    Only to God and to those

Who, being soulless, are free from shame,
    Whatever meat they may find.
Nor do they defile the dead man's name—
    That is reserved for his kind.

D. H. LAWRENCE (1885–1930)

from EAGLE IN NEW MEXICO

Towards the sun, towards the south-west
A scorched breast.
A scorched breast, breasting the sun like an answer,
Like a retort.

An eagle at the top of a low cedar-bush
On the sage-ash desert
Reflecting the scorch of the sun from his breast;
Eagle, with the sickle dripping darkly above.

Erect, scorched-pallid out of the hair of the cedar,
Erect, with the god-thrust entering him from below,
Eagle gloved in feathers
In scorched white feathers
In burnt dark feathers
In feathers still fire-rusted;
Sickle-overswept, sickle dripping over and above.

Sun-breaster,
Staring two ways at once, to right and left;
Masked-one
Dark-visaged
Sickle-masked
With iron between your two eyes;
You feather-gloved
To the feet;
Foot-fierce;
Erect onel;
The god-thrust entering you steadily from below.

You never look at the sun with your two eyes.
Only the inner eye of your scorched broad breast
Looks straight at the sun.

You are dark
Except scorch-pale-breasted;
And dark cleaves down and weapon-hard downward curving
At your scorched breast,
Like a sword of Damocles,
Beaked eagle.

You've dipped it in blood so many times
That dark face-weapon, to temper it well,
Blood-thirsty bird.

ALFRED, LORD TENNYSON (1809–92)

THE EAGLE
Fragment

He clasps the crag with crooked hands;
Close to the sun in lonely lands,
Ringed with the azure world, he stands.

The wrinkled sea beneath him crawls;
He watches from his mountain walls,
And like a thunderbolt he falls.

HILAIRE BELLOC (1870–1953)

THE VULTURE

The Vulture eats between his meals
    And that's the reason why
He very, very rarely feels
    As well as you and I.

His eye is dull, his head is bald,
    His neck is growing thinner.
Oh! what a lesson for us all
    To only eat at dinner!

TED HUGHES (1930–98)

HAWK ROOSTING

I sit in the top of the wood, my eyes closed.
Inaction, no falsifying dream
Between my hooked head and hooked feet:
Or in sleep rehearse perfect kills and eat.

The convenience of the high trees!
The air's buoyancy and the sun's ray
Are of advantage to me;
And the earth's face upward for my inspection.

My feet are locked upon the rough bark.
It took the whole of Creation
To produce my foot, my each feather:
Now I hold Creation in my foot

Or fly up, and revolve it all slowly —
I kill where I please because it is all mine.
There is no sophistry in my body:
My manners are tearing off heads —

The allotment of death.
For the one path of my flight is direct
Through the bones of the living.
No arguments assert my right:

The sun is behind me.
Nothing has changed since I began.
My eye has permitted no change.
I am going to keep things like this.

GEORGE MACBETH (1932–92)

OWL

is my favourite. Who flies
like a nothing through the night,
who-whoing. Is a feather
duster in leafy corners ring-a-rosy-ing
boles of mice. Twice

you hear him call. Who
is he looking for? You hear
him hoovering over the floor
of the wood. O would you be gold
rings in the driving skull

if you could? Hooded and
vulnerable by the winter suns
owl looks. Is the grain of bark
in the dark. Round beaks are at
work in the pellety nest,

resting. Owl is an eye
in the barn. For a hole
in the trunk owl's blood
is to blame. Black talons in the
petrified fur! Cold walnut hands

on the case of the brain! In the reign
of the chicken owl comes like
a god. Is a goad in
the rain to the pink eyes,
dripping. For a meal in the day

flew, killed, on the moor. Six
mouths are the seed of his
arc in the season. Torn meat
from the sky. Owl lives
by the claws of his brain. On the branch

in the sever of the hand's
twigs owl is a backward look.
Flown wind in the skin. Fine
rain in the bones. Owl breaks
like the day. Am an owl, am an owl.

TED HUGHES (1930–98)

THRUSHES

Terrifying are the attent sleek thrushes on the lawn,
More coiled steel than living—a poised
Dark deadly eye, those delicate legs
Triggered to stirrings beyond sense—with a start, a bounce, a stab
Overtake the instant and drag out some writhing thing.
No indolent procrastinations and no yawning stares,
No sighs or head-scratchings. Nothing but bounce and stab
And a ravening second.

Is it their single-mind-sized skulls, or a trained
Body, or genius, or a nestful of brats
Gives their days this bullet and automatic
Purpose? Mozart's brain had it, and the shark's mouth
That hungers down the blood-smell even to a leak of its own
Side and devouring of itself: efficiency which
Strikes too streamlined for any doubt to pluck at it
Or obstruction deflect.

With a man it is otherwise. Heroisms on horseback,
Outstripping his desk-diary at a broad desk,
Carving at a tiny ivory ornament
For years: his act worships itself—while for him,
Though he bends to be blent in the prayer, how loud and above what

Furious spaces of fire do the distracting devils
Orgy and hosannah, under what wilderness
Of black silent waters weep.

ANON

---

from BEOWULF

Then a powerful demon, a prowler through the dark,
nursed a hard grievance. It harrowed him
to hear the din of the loud banquet
every day in the hall, the harp being struck
and the clear song of a skilled poet
telling with mastery of man's beginnings,
how the Almighty had made the earth
a gleaming plain girdled with waters;
in His splendour He set the sun and the moon
to be earth's lamplight, lanterns for men,
and filled the broad lap of the world
with branches and leaves; and quickened life
in every other thing that moved.

So times were pleasant for the people there
until finally one, a fiend out of hell,
began to work his evil in the world.
Grendel was the name of this grim demon
haunting the marches, marauding round the heath
and the desolate fens; he had dwelt for a time
in misery among the banished monsters,
Cain's clan, whom the Creator had outlawed
and condemned as outcasts. For the killing of Abel
the Eternal Lord had exacted a price:
Cain got no good from committing that murder
because the Almighty made him anathema
and out of the curse of his exile there sprang
orgres and elves and evil phantoms
and the giants too who strove with God
time and again until He gave them their reward.

So, after nightfall, Grendel set out
for the lofty house, to see how the Ring-Danes
were settling into it after their drink,

and there he came upon them, a company of the best
asleep from their feasting, insensible to pain
and human sorrow. Suddenly then
the God-cursed brute was creating havoc:
greedy and grim, he grabbed thirty men
from their resting places and rushed to his lair,
flushed up and inflamed from the raid,
blundering back with the butchered corpses.

Then as dawn brightened and the day broke
Grendel's powers of destruction were plain:
their wassail was over, they wept to heaven
and mourned under morning.

LEWIS CARROLL (1832–98)

JABBERWOCKY

'Twas brillig, and the slithy toves
　　Did gyre and gimble in the wabe:
All mimsy were the borogoves,
　　And the mome raths outgrabe.

"Beware the Jabberwock, my son!
　　The jaws that bite, the claws that catch!
Beware the Jubjub bird, and shun
　　The frumious Bandersnatch!"

He took his vorpal sword in hand:
　　Long time the manxome foe he sought—
So rested he by the Tumtum tree,
　　And stood awhile in thought.

And, as in uffish thought he stood,
　　The Jabberwock, with eyes of flame,
Came whiffling through the tulgey wood,
　　And burbled as it came!

One, two! One, two! And through and through
　　The vorpal blade went snicker-snack!
He left it dead, and with its head
　　He went galumphing back.

"And hast thou slain the Jabberwock?
　　Come to my arms, my beamish boy!
O frabjous day! Callooh! Callay!"
　　He chortled in his joy.

'Twas brillig, and the slithy toves
　　Did gyre and gimble in the wabe:
All mimsy were the borogoves,
　　And the mome raths outgrabe.

ALFRED, LORD TENNYSON (1809–92)

THE KRAKEN

Below the thunders of the upper deep;
Far, far beneath in the abysmal sea,
His ancient, dreamless, uninvaded sleep
The Kraken sleepeth: faintest sunlights flee
About his shadowy sides: above him swell
Huge sponges of millennial growth and height;
And far away into the sickly light,
From many a wondrous grot and secret cell
Unnumbered and enormous polypi
Winnow with giant fins the slumbering green.
There hath he lain for ages and will lie
Battening upon huge seaworms in his sleep,
Until the latter fire shall heat the deep;
Then once by men and angels to be seen,
In roaring he shall rise and on the surface die.

HERMAN MELVILLE (1819–91)

THE MALDIVE SHARK

About the Shark, phlegmatical one,
Pale sot of the Maldive sea,
The sleek little pilot-fish, azure and slim,
How alert in attendance be.
From his saw-pit of mouth, from his charnel of maw,
They have nothing of harm to dread,
But liquidly glide on his ghastly flank
Or before his Gorgonian head;
Or lurk in the port of serrated teeth
In white triple tiers of glittering gates,
And there find a haven when peril's abroad,
An asylum in jaws of the Fates!

They are friends; and friendly they guide him to prey,
Yet never partake of the treat—
Eyes and brains to the dotard lethargic and dull,
Pale ravener of horrible meat.

EDMUND BLUNDEN (1896–1974)

THE PIKE

From shadows of rich oaks outpeer
The moss-green bastions of the weir,
Where the quick dipper forages
In elver-peopled crevices,
And a small runlet trickling down the sluice
Gossamer music tires not to unloose.

Else round the broad pool's hush
Nothing stirs,
Unless sometimes a straggling heifer crush
Through the thronged spinney where the pheasant whirs;

Or martins in a flash
Come with wild mirth to dip their magical wings,
While in the shallow some doomed bulrush swings
At whose hid root the diver vole's teeth gnash.

And nigh this toppling reed, still as the dead
The great pike lies, the murderous patriarch
Watching the waterpit sheer-shelving dark,
Where through the plash his lithe bright vassals thread.

The rose-finned roach and bluish bream
And staring ruffe steal up the stream
Hard by their glutted tyrant, now
Still as a sunken bough.

He on the sandbank lies,
Sunning himself long hours
With stony gorgon eyes:
Westward the hot sun lowers.

Sudden the gray pike changes, and quivering poises for
   slaughter;
        Intense terror wakens around him, the shoals scud
          awry, but there chances
        A chub unsuspecting; the prowling fins quicken, in
          fury he lances;
And the miller that opens the hatch stands amazed at the whirl
   in the water.

JAMES FENTON (1949–)

THE KILLER SNAILS

The killer snails
Have slung their silver trails
Along the doormat, out across the lawn,
Under the bushes
Where the alarming thrushes
Give night its notice, making way for dawn,
And the obliging lizards drop their tails.

On webs of dew
The spiders stir their pots of glue
And drag their quartered victims to the shade.
Soaked in their rugs
Of grass and moss the slugs
Wind up another night of sluggish trade
And young ingredients get into a stew.

The sorrel bends.
The path fades out but never ends
Where brambles clutch and bracken wipes your feet.
It goes in rings.
Its mind's on other things.
Its way and its intentions never meet.
Meetings of friends?
It gives no undertaking. It depends.

ROBERT FROST (1874–1963)

DESIGN

I found a dimpled spider, fat and white,
On a white heal-all, holding up a moth
Like a white piece of rigid satin cloth—
Assorted characters of death and blight
Mixed ready to begin the morning right,
Like the ingredients of a witches' broth—
A snow-drop spider, a flower like a froth,
And dead wings carried like a paper kite.

What had that flower to do with being white,
The wayside blue and innocent heal-all?
What brought the kindred spider to that height,
Then steered the white moth thither in the night?
What but design of darkness to appall?—
If design govern in a thing so small.

'All things innocent, hapless, forsaken.'
from 'The Meadow Mouse'

THEODORE ROETHKE (1908–63)

THE MEADOW MOUSE

I

In a shoe box stuffed in an old nylon stocking
Sleeps the baby mouse I found in the meadow,
Where he trembled and shook beneath a stick
Till I caught him up by the tail and brought him in,
Cradled in my hand,
A little quaker, the whole body of him trembling,
His absurd whiskers sticking out like a cartoon-mouse,
His feet like small leaves,
Little lizard-feet,
Whitish and spread wide when he tried to struggle away,
Wriggling like a minuscule puppy.

Now he's eaten his three kinds of cheese and drunk from his
    bottle-cap watering-trough—
So much he just lies in one corner,
His tail curled under him, his belly big
As his head, his bat-like ears
Twitching, tilting toward the least sound.

Do I imagine he no longer trembles
When I come close to him?
He seems no longer to tremble.

II

But this morning the shoe-box house on the back porch is empty.
Where has he gone, my meadow mouse,
My thumb of a child that nuzzled in my palm?—

To run under the hawk's wing,
Under the eye of the great owl watching from the elm-tree,
To live by courtesy of the shrike, the snake, the tom-cat.

I think of the nestling fallen into the deep grass,
The turtle gasping in the dusty rubble of the highway,
The paralytic stunned in the tub, and the water rising,—
All things innocent, hapless, forsaken.

W. B. YEATS (1865–1939)

'LONELY THE SEA-BIRD LIES AT HER REST'
from SONG FOR THE CLOTH: *CALVARY*

Lonely the sea-bird lies at her rest,
Blown like a dawn-blenched parcel of spray
Upon the wind, or follows her prey
Under a great wave's hollowing crest.

God has not appeared to the birds.

The ger-eagle has chosen his part
In blue-deep of the upper air
Where one-eyed day can meet his stare;
He is content with his savage heart.

God has not appeared to the birds.

But where have last-year's cygnets gone?
The lake is empty; why do they fling
White wing out beside white wing?
What can a swan need but a swan?

God has not appeared to the birds.

GEORGE MACKAY BROWN (1921–96)

THE HAWK

On Sunday the hawk fell on Bigging
And a chicken screamed
Lost in its own little snowstorm.
And on Monday he fell on the moor
And the Field Club
Raised a hundred silent prisms.
And on Tuesday he fell on the hill
And the happy lamb
Never knew why the loud collie straddled him.
And on Wednesday he fell on a bush
And the blackbird
Laid by his little flute for the last time.
And on Thursday he fell on Cleat
And peerie Tom's rabbit
Swung in a single arc from shore to hill.
And on Friday he fell on a ditch
But the rampant rat,
That eye and that tooth, quenched his flame.
And on Saturday he fell on Bigging
And Jock lowered his gun
And nailed a small wing over the corn.

THOMAS LOVELL BEDDOES (1803–49)

A CROCODILE

Hard by the lilied Nile I saw
A duskish river dragon stretched along.
The brown habergeon of his limbs enamelled
With sanguine alamandines and rainy pearl:
And on his back there lay a young one sleeping,
No bigger than a mouse; with eyes like beads,
And a small fragment of its speckled egg
Remaining on its harmless, pulpy snout;

A thing to laugh at, as it gaped to catch
The baulking merry flies. In the iron jaws
Of the great devil-beast, like a pale soul
Fluttering in rocky hell, lightsomely flew
A snowy trochilus, with roseate beak
Tearing the hairy leeches from his throat.

WILLIAM BLAKE (1757–1827)

THE FLY

Little Fly
Thy summers play,
My thoughtless hand
Has brush'd away.

Am not I
A fly like thee?
Or art not thou
A man like me?

For I dance
And drink & sing:
Till some blind hand
Shall brush my wing.

If thought is life
And strength & breath:
And the want
Of thought is death;

Then am I
A happy fly,
If I live,
Or if I die.

ANDREW YOUNG (1885–1971)

THE DEAD CRAB

A rosy shield upon its back,
That not the hardest storm could crack,
From whose sharp edge projected out
Black pinpoint eyes staring about;
Beneath, the well-knit cote-armure
That gave to its weak belly power;
The clustered legs with plated joints
That ended in stiletto points;
The claws like mouths it held outside:
I cannot think this creature died
By storm or fish or sea-fowl harmed
Walking the sea so heavily armed;
Or does it make for death to be
Oneself a living armoury?

TED HUGHES (1930–98)

AN OTTER

I

Underwater eyes, an eel's
Oil of water body, neither fish nor beast is the otter:
    Four-legged yet water-gifted, to outfish fish;
        With webbed feet and long ruddering tail
        And a round head like an old tomcat.

    Brings the legend of himself
From before wars or burials, in spite of hounds and vermin-poles;
    Does not take root like the badger. Wanders, cries;
        Gallops along land he no longer belongs to;
        Re-enters the water by melting.

        Of neither water nor land. Seeking
Some world lost when first he dived, that he cannot come at since,
    Takes his changed body into the holes of lakes;
        As if blind, cleaves the stream's push till he licks
        The pebbles of the source; from sea

    To sea crosses in three nights
Like a king in hiding. Crying to the old shape of the starlit land,
    Over sunken farms where the bats go round,
        Without answer. Till light and birdsong come
        Walloping up roads with the milk wagon.

II

The hunt's lost him. Pads on mud,
Among sedges, nostrils a surface bead,
The otter remains, hours. The air,
Circling the globe, tainted and necessary,

Mingling tobacco-smoke, hounds and parsley,
Comes carefully to the sunk lungs.
So the self under the eye lies,
Attendant and withdrawn. The otter belongs

In double robbery and concealment—
From water that nourishes and drowns, and from land
That gave him his length and the mouth of the hound.
He keeps fat in the limpid integument

Reflections live on. The heart beats thick,
Big trout muscle out of the dead cold;
Blood is the belly of logic; he will lick
The fishbone bare. And can take stolen hold

On a bitch otter in a field full
Of nervous horses, but linger nowhere.
Yanked above hounds, reverts to nothing at all,
To this long pelt over the back of a chair.

JOHN CLARE (1793–1864)

THE BADGER

The badger grunting on his woodland track
With shaggy hide and sharp nose scrowed with black
Roots in the bushes and the woods and makes
A great hugh burrow in the ferns and brakes
With nose on ground he runs a awkard pace
And anything will beat him in the race
The shepherds dog will run him to his den
Followed and hooted by the dogs and men
The woodman when the hunting comes about
Go round at night to stop the foxes out
And hurrying through the bushes ferns and brakes
Nor sees the many hol[e]s the badger makes
And often through the bushes to the chin
Breaks the old holes and tumbles headlong in

When midnight comes a host of dogs and men
Go out and track the badger to his den
And put a sack within the hole and lye
Till the old grunting badger passes bye
He comes and hears they let the strongest loose
The old fox hears the noise and drops the goose
The poacher shoots and hurrys from the cry
And the old hare half wounded buzzes bye
They get a forked stick to bear him down
And clapt the dogs and bore him to the town
And bait him all the day with many dogs
And laugh and shout and fright the scampering hogs
He runs along and bites at all he meets
They shout and hollo down the noisey streets

He turns about to face the loud uproar
And drives the rebels to their very doors
The frequent stone is hurled where ere they go
When badgers fight and every ones a foe

The dogs are clapt and urged to join the fray
The badger turns and drives them all away
Though scar[c]ely half as big dimute and small
He fights with dogs for hours and beats them all
The heavy mastiff savage in the fray
Lies down and licks his feet and turns away
The bull dog knows his match and waxes cold
The badger grins and never leaves his hold
He drive[s] the crowd and follows at their heels
And bites them through the drunkard swears and reels

The frighted women takes the boys away
The blackguard laughs and hurrys on the fray
He try to reach the woods a awkard race
But sticks and cudgels quickly stop the chace
He turns agen and drives the noisey crowd
And beats the many dogs in noises loud
He drives away and beats them every one
And then they loose them all and set them on
He falls as dead and kicked by boys and men
Then starts and grins and drives the crowd agen
Till kicked and torn and beaten out he lies
And leaves his hold and cackles groans and dies

Some keep a baited badger tame as hog
And tame him till he follows like the dog
They urge him on like dogs and show fair play
He beats and scarcely wounded goes away
Lapt up as if asleep he scorns to fly
And siezes any dog that ventures nigh
Clapt like a dog he never bites the men
But worrys dogs and hurrys to his den
They let him out and turn a barrow down
And there he fights the host of all the town

101

He licks the patting hand and trys to play
And never trys to bite or run away
And runs away from noise in hollow tree[s]
Burnt by the boys to get a swarm of bees

'there trembled through
His happy goodnight air
Some blessed Hope, whereof he knew
And I was unaware.'

from 'The Darkling Thrush'

PERCY BYSSHE SHELLEY (1792–1822)

TO A SKYLARK

Hail to thee, blithe Spirit!
   Bird thou never wert,
That from Heaven, or near it,
   Pourest thy full heart
In profuse strains of unpremeditated art.

Higher still and higher
   From the earth thou springest
Like a cloud of fire;
   The blue deep thou wingest,
And singing still dost soar, and soaring ever singest.

In the golden lightning
   Of the sunken sun,
O'er which clouds are bright'ning,
   Thou dost float and run;
Like an unbodied joy whose race is just begun.

The pale purple even
   Melts around thy flight;
Like a star of Heaven,
   In the broad daylight
Thou art unseen, but yet I hear thy shrill delight,

Keen as are the arrows
   Of that silver sphere,
Whose intense lamp narrows
   In the white dawn clear
Until we hardly see—we feel that it is there.

All the earth and air
   With thy voice is loud,
As, when night is bare,
   From one lonely cloud
The moon rains out her beams, and Heaven is overflowed.

What thou art we know not;
  What is most like thee?
From rainbow clouds there flow not
  Drops so bright to see
As from thy presence showers a rain of melody.

Like a Poet hidden
  In the light of thought,
Singing hymns unbidden,
  Till the world is wrought
To sympathy with hopes and fears it heeded not:

Like a high-born maiden
  In a palace tower,
Soothing her love-laden
  Soul in secret hour
With music sweet as love, which overflows her bower:

Like a glowworm golden
  In a dell of dew,
Scattering unbeholden
  Its aërial hue
Among the flowers and grass, which screen it from the view!

Like a rose embowered
  In its own green leaves,
By warm winds deflowered,
  Till the scent it gives
Makes faint with too much sweet those heavy-wingéd thieves:

Sound of vernal showers
  On the twinkling grass,
Rain-awakened flowers,
  All that ever was
Joyous, and clear, and fresh, thy music doth surpass:

Teach us, Sprite or Bird,
    What sweet thoughts are thine:
I have never heard
    Praise of love or wine
That panted forth a flood of rapture so divine.

Chorus Hymeneal,
    Or triumphal chant,
Matched with thine would be all
    But an empty vaunt,
A thing wherein we feel there is some hidden want.

What objects are the fountains
    Of thy happy strain?
What fields, or waves, or mountains?
    What shapes of sky or plain?
What love of thine own kind? what ignorance of pain?

With thy clear keen joyance
    Languor cannot be:
Shadow of annoyance
    Never came near thee:
Thou lovest—but ne'er knew love's sad satiety.

Waking or asleep,
    Thou of death must deem
Things more true and deep
    Than we mortals dream,
Or how could thy notes flow in such a crystal stream?

We look before and after,
    And pine for what is not:
Our sincerest laughter
    With some pain is fraught;
Our sweetest songs are those that tell of saddest thought.

Yet if we could scorn
        Hate, and pride, and fear;
If we were things born
        Not to shed a tear,
I know not how thy joy we ever should come near.

Better than all measures
        Of delightful sound,
Better than all treasures
        That in books are found,
Thy skill to poet were, thou scorner of the ground!

Teach me half the gladness
        That thy brain must know,
Such harmonious madness
        From my lips would flow
The world should listen then—as I am listening now.

THOMAS HARDY (1840–1928)

THE DARKLING THRUSH

I leant upon a coppice gate
   When Frost was spectre-gray,
And Winter's dregs made desolate
   The weakening eye of day.
The tangled bine-stems scored the sky
   Like strings of broken lyres,
And all mankind that haunted nigh
   Had sought their household fires.

The land's sharp features seemed to be
   The Century's corpse outleant,
His crypt the cloudy canopy,
   The wind his death-lament.
The ancient pulse of germ and birth
   Was shrunken hard and dry,
And every spirit upon earth
   Seemed fervourless as I.

At once a voice arose among
   The bleak twigs overhead
In a full-hearted evensong
   Of joy illimited;
An aged thrush, frail, gaunt, and small,
   In blast-beruffled plume,
Had chosen thus to fling his soul
   Upon the growing gloom.

So little cause for carolings
   Of such ecstatic sound
Was written on terrestrial things
   Afar or nigh around,
That I could think there trembled through
   His happy goodnight air
Some blessed Hope, whereof he knew
   And I was unaware.

ANON
___

CUCKOO SONG

Summer is y-comen in,
    Loude sing, cuckoo!
Groweth seed and bloweth meed
    And spring'th the woode now —
      Sing cuckoo!

Ewe bleateth after lamb,
    Low'th after calfe cow;
Bullock starteth, bucke farteth.
    Merry sing, cuckoo!

    Cuckoo, Cuckoo!
Well sing'st thou, cuckoo:
    Ne swike thou never now!

Sing cuckoo, now! Sing, cuckoo!
Sing cuckoo! Sing, cuckoo, now!

WILLIAM WORDSWORTH (1770–1850)

TO THE CUCKOO

O blithe New-comer! I have heard,
I hear thee and rejoice.
O Cuckoo! shall I call thee Bird,
Or but a wandering Voice?

While I am lying on the grass
Thy twofold shout I hear;
From hill to hill it seems to pass
At once far off, and near.

Though babbling only to the Vale,
Of sunshine and of flowers,
Thou bringest unto me a tale
Of visionary hours.

Thrice welcome, darling of the Spring!
Even yet thou art to me
No bird, but an invisible thing,
A voice, a mystery;

The same whom in my schoolboy days
I listened to; that Cry
Which made me look a thousand ways
In bush, and tree, and sky.

To seek thee did I often rove
Through woods and on the green;
And thou wert still a hope, a love;
Still longed for, never seen.

And I can listen to thee yet;
Can lie upon the plain
And listen, till I do beget
That golden time again.

O blessed Bird! the earth we pace
Again appears to be
An unsubstantial, faery place;
That is fit home for Thee!

STEVIE SMITH (1902–71)

THE SINGING CAT

It was a little captive cat
    Upon a crowded train
His mistress takes him from his box
    To ease his fretful pain.

She holds him tight upon her knee
    The graceful animal
And all the people look at him
    He is so beautiful.

But oh he pricks and oh he prods
    And turns upon her knee
Then lifteth up his innocent voice
    In plaintive melody.

He lifteth up his innocent voice
    He lifteth up, he singeth
And to each human countenance
    A smile of grace he bringeth.

He lifteth up his innocent paw
    Upon her breast he clingeth
And everybody cries, Behold
    The cat, the cat that singeth.

He lifteth up his innocent voice
    He lifteth up, he singeth
And all the people warm themselves
    In the love his beauty bringeth.

JOHN KEATS (1795–1821)

ODE TO A NIGHTINGALE

1

My heart aches, and a drowsy numbness pains
   My sense, as though of hemlock I had drunk,
Or emptied some dull opiate to the drains
   One minute past, and Lethe-wards had sunk:
'Tis not through envy of thy happy lot,
   But being too happy in thine happiness—
      That thou, light-wingéd Dryad of the trees,
        In some melodious plot
   Of beechen green, and shadows numberless,
      Singest of summer in full-throated ease.

2

O, for a draught of vintage! that hath been
   Cooled a long age in the deep-delvéd earth,
Tasting of Flora and the country green,
   Dance, and Provençal song, and sunburnt mirth!
O for a beaker full of the warm South,
   Full of the true, the blushful Hippocrene,
      With beaded bubbles winking at the brim,
        And purple-stainéd mouth;
   That I might drink, and leave the world unseen,
      And with thee fade away into the forest dim:

3

Fade far away, dissolve, and quite forget
   What thou among the leaves hast never known,
The weariness, the fever, and the fret
   Here, where men sit and hear each other groan;
Where palsy shakes a few, sad, last gray hairs,
   Where youth grows pale, and spectre-thin, and dies,
   Where but to think is to be full of sorrow

And leaden-eyed despairs,
Where Beauty cannot keep her lustrous eyes,
Or new Love pine at them beyond tomorrow.

4

Away! away! for I will fly to thee,
Not charioted by Bacchus and his pards,
But on the viewless wings of Poesy,
Though the dull brain perplexes and retards:
Already with thee! tender is the night,
And haply the Queen-Moon is on her throne,
Clustered around by all her starry Fays;
But here there is no light,
Save what from heaven is with the breezes blown
Through verdurous glooms and winding mossy ways.

5

I cannot see what flowers are at my feet,
Nor what soft incense hangs upon the boughs,
But, in embalmèd darkness, guess each sweet
Wherewith the seasonable month endows
The grass, the thicket, and the fruit tree wild;
White hawthorn, and the pastoral eglantine;
Fast fading violets covered up in leaves;
And mid-May's eldest child,
The coming musk-rose, full of dewy wine,
The murmurous haunt of flies on summer eves.

6

Darkling I listen; and for many a time
I have been half in love with easeful Death,
Called him soft names in many a musèd rhyme,

To take into the air my quiet breath;
Now more than ever seems it rich to die,
To cease upon the midnight with no pain,
While thou art pouring forth thy soul abroad
In such an ecstasy!
Still wouldst thou sing, and I have ears in vain—
To thy high requiem become a sod.

7

Thou wast not born for death, immortal Bird!
No hungry generations tread thee down;
The voice I hear this passing night was heard
In ancient days by emperor and clown:
Perhaps the selfsame song that found a path
Through the sad heart of Ruth, when, sick for home,
She stood in tears amid the alien corn;
The same that ofttimes hath
Charmed magic casements, opening on the foam
Of perilous seas, in faery lands forlorn.

8

Forlorn! the very word is like a bell
To toll me back from thee to my sole self!
Adieu! the fancy cannot cheat so well
As she is famed to do, deceiving elf.
Adieu! adieu! thy plaintive anthem fades
Past the near meadows, over the still stream,
Up the hill side; and now 'tis buried deep
In the next valley-glades:
Was it a vision, or a waking dream?
Fled is that music:—Do I wake or sleep?

EDWARD THOMAS (1878–1917)

THE UNKNOWN BIRD

Three lovely notes he whistled, too soft to be heard
If others sang; but others never sang
In the great beech-wood all that May and June.
No one saw him: I alone could hear him
Though many listened. Was it but four years
Ago? or five? He never came again.

Oftenest when I heard him I was alone,
Nor could I ever make another hear.
La-la-la! he called, seeming far off—
As if a cock crowed past the edge of the world,
As if the bird or I were in a dream.
Yet that he travelled through the trees and sometimes
Neared me, was plain, though somehow distant still
He sounded. All the proof is—I told men
What I had heard.

                I never knew a voice,
Man, beast, or bird, better than this. I told
The naturalists; but neither had they heard
Anything like the notes that did so haunt me;
I had them clear by heart and have them still.
Four years, or five, have made no difference. Then
As now that La-la-la! was bodiless sweet:
Sad more than joyful it was, if I must say
That it was one or other, but if sad
'Twas sad only with joy too, too far off
For me to taste it. But I cannot tell
If truly never anything but fair
The days were when he sang, as now they seem.
This surely I know, that I who listened then,
Happy sometimes, sometimes suffering
A heavy body and a heavy heart,
Now straightway, if I think of it, become
Light as that bird wandering beyond my shore.

WILLIAM WORDSWORTH (1770–1850)

THE GREEN LINNET

Beneath these fruit-tree boughs that shed
Their snow-white blossoms on my head,
With brightest sunshine round me spread
   Of spring's unclouded weather,
In this sequestered nook how sweet
To sit upon my orchard-seat!
And birds and flowers once more to greet,
   My last year's friends together.

One have I marked, the happiest guest
In all this covert of the blest:
Hail to Thee, far above the rest
   In joy of voice and pinion!
Thou, Linnet! in thy green array,
Presiding Spirit here to-day,
Dost lead the revels of the May;
   And this is thy dominion.

While birds, and butterflies, and flowers,
Make all one band of paramours,
Thou, ranging up and down the bowers,
   Art sole in thy employment:
A Life, a Presence like the Air,
Scattering thy gladness without care,
Too blest with any one to pair:
   Thyself thy own enjoyment.

Amid yon tuft of hazel trees,
That twinkle to the gusty breeze,
Behold him perched in ecstasies,
   Yet seeming still to hover;
There! where the flutter of his wings
Upon his back and body flings
Shadows and sunny glimmerings,
   That cover him all over.

My dazzled sight he oft deceives,
A Brother of the dancing leaves;
Then flits, and from the cottage eaves
  Pours forth his song in gushes;
As if by that exulting strain
He mocked and treated with disdain
The voiceless Form he chose to feign,
  While fluttering in the bushes.

GERARD MANLEY HOPKINS (1844–89)

THE WINDHOVER
To Christ Our Lord

I caught this morning morning's minion,
   kingdom of daylight's dauphin, dapple-dawn-drawn Falcon,
     in his riding
   Of the rolling level underneath him steady air, and striding
High there, how he rung upon the rein of a wimpling wing
In his ecstasy! then off, off forth on swing,
   As a skate's heel sweeps smooth on a bow-bend: the hurl and
     gliding
   Rebuffed the big wind. My heart in hiding
Stirred for a bird,— the achieve of, the mastery of the thing!

Brute beauty and valour and act, oh, air, pride, plume, here
   Buckle! and the fire that breaks from thee then, a billion
Times told lovelier, more dangerous, O my chevalier!
   No wonder of it: shéer plód makes plough down sillion
Shine, and blue-beak embers, ah my dear,
   Fall, gall themselves, and gash gold-vermilion.

WILLIAM WORDSWORTH (1770–1850)

TO A BUTTERFLY

Stay near me—do not take thy flight!
A little longer stay in sight!
Much converse do I find in thee,
Historian of my infancy!
Float near me; do not yet depart!
Dead times revive in thee:
Thou bring'st, gay creature as thou art!
A solemn image to my heart,
My father's family!

Oh! pleasant, pleasant were the days,
The time, when in our childish plays,
My sister Emmeline and I
Together chased the butterfly!
A very hunter did I rush
Upon the prey;— with leaps and springs
I followed on from brake to bush;
But she, God love her! feared to brush
The dust from off its wings.

EDWARD THOMAS (1878–1917)

THE OWL

Downhill I came, hungry, and yet not starved;
Cold, yet had heat within me that was proof
Against the North wind; tired, yet so that rest
Had seemed the sweetest thing under a roof.

Then at the inn I had food, fire, and rest,
Knowing how hungry, cold, and tired was I.
All of the night was quite barred out except
An owl's cry, a most melancholy cry

Shaken out long and clear upon the hill,
No merry note, nor cause of merriment,
But one telling me plain what I escaped
And others could not, that night, as in I went.

And salted was my food, and my repose,
Salted and sobered, too, by the bird's voice
Speaking for all who lay under the stars,
Soldiers and poor, unable to rejoice.

ROBERT FROST (1874–1963)

DUST OF SNOW

The way a crow
Shook down on me
The dust of snow
From a hemlock tree

Has given my heart
A change of mood
And saved some part
Of a day I had rued.

SYLVIA PLATH (1932–63)

BLACK ROOK IN RAINY WEATHER

On the stiff twig up there
Hunches a wet black rook
Arranging and rearranging its feathers in the rain.
I do not expect miracle
Or an accident

To set the sight on fire
In my eye, nor seek
Any more in the desultory weather some design,
But let spotted leaves fall as they fall,
Without ceremony, or portent

Although, I admit, I desire,
Occasionally, some backtalk
From the mute sky, I can't honestly complain:
A certain minor light may still
Leap incandescent

Out of kitchen table or chair
As if a celestial burning took
Possession of the most obtuse objects now and then—
Thus hallowing an interval
Otherwise inconsequent

By bestowing largesse, honor,
One might say love. At any rate, I now walk
Wary (for it could happen
Even in this dull, ruinous landscape); skeptical,
Yet politic; ignorant

Of whatever angel may choose to flare
Suddenly at my elbow. I only know that a rook
Ordering its black feathers can so shine
As to seize my senses, haul
My eyelids up, and grant

A brief respite from fear
Of total neutrality. With luck,
Trekking stubborn through this season
Of fatigue, I shall
Patch together a content

Of sorts. Miracles occur,
If you care to call those spasmodic
Tricks of radiance miracles. The wait's begun again,
The long wait for the angel,
For that rare, random descent.

TED HUGHES (1930–98)

THE THOUGHT-FOX

I imagine this midnight moment's forest:
Something else is alive
Beside the clock's loneliness
And this blank page where my fingers move.

Through the window I see no star:
Something more near
Though deeper within darkness
Is entering the loneliness:

Cold, delicately as the dark snow,
A fox's nose touches twig, leaf;
Two eyes serve a moment, that now
And again now, and now, and now

Sets neat prints into the snow
Between trees, and warily a lame
Shadow lags by stump and in hollow
Of a body that is bold to come

Across clearings, an eye,
A widening deepening greenness,
Brilliantly, concentratedly,
Coming about its own business

Till, with a sudden sharp hot stink of fox
It enters the dark hole of the head.
The window is starless still; the clock ticks,
The page is printed.

THOMAS HARDY (1840–1928)

THE FALLOW DEER AT THE LONELY HOUSE

One without looks in tonight
    Through the curtain-chink
From the sheet of glistening white;
One without looks in tonight
    As we sit and think
    By the fender-brink.

We do not discern those eyes
    Watching in the snow;
Lit by lamps of rosy dyes
We do not discern those eyes
    Wondering, aglow,
    Fourfooted, tiptoe.

NORMAN MACCAIG (1910–96)

TOAD

Stop looking like a purse. How could a purse
squeeze under the rickety door and sit,
full of satisfaction, in a man's house?

You clamber towards me on your four corners—
right hand, left foot, left hand, right foot.

I love you for being a toad,
for crawling like a Japanese wrestler,
and for not being frightened.

I put you in my purse hand, not shutting it,
and set you down outside directly under
every star.

A jewel in your head? Toad,
you've put one in mine,
a tiny radiance in a dark place.

'This Chanticleer stood high upon his toes,
He stretched his neck, his eyes began to close,
His beak to open;'

from 'The Nun's Priest's Tale'

WILLIAM SHAKESPEARE (1564–1616)

THE PHOENIX AND THE TURTLE

Let the bird of loudest lay
On the sole Arabian tree
Herald sad and trumpet be,
To whose sound chaste wings obey.

But thou shrieking harbinger,
Foul precurrer of the fiend,
Augur of the fever's end,
To this troop come thou not near.

From this session interdict
Every fowl of tyrant wing,
Save the eagle, feath'red king:
Keep the obsequy so strict.

Let the priest in surplice white,
That defunctive music can,
Be the death-divining swan,
Lest the requiem lack his right.

And thou treble-dated crow,
That thy sable gender mak'st
With the breath thou giv'st and tak'st,
'Mongst our mourners shalt thou go.

Here the anthem doth commence:
Love and constancy is dead,
Phoenix and the turtle fled
In a mutual flame from hence.

So they loved, as love in twain
Had the essence but in one;
Two distincts, division none:
Number there in love was slain.

Hearts remote, yet not asunder;
Distance and no space was seen
'Twixt this turtle and his queen;
But in them it were a wonder.

So between them love did shine
That the turtle saw his right
Flaming in the phoenix' sight:
Either was the other's mine.

Property was thus appallèd,
That the self was not the same;
Single nature's double name
Neither two nor one was callèd.

Reason, in itself confounded,
Saw division grow together,
To themselves yet either neither,
Simple were so well compounded;

That it cried, 'How true a twain
Seemeth this concordant one!
Love hath reason, reason none,
If what parts can so remain.'

Whereupon it made this threne
To the phoenix and the dove,
Co-supremes and stars of love,
As chorus to their tragic scene.

THRENOS

Beauty, truth, and rarity,
Grace in all simplicity,
Here enclosed, in cinders lie.

Death is now the phoenix' nest,
And the turtle's loyal breast
To eternity doth rest,

Leaving no posterity:
'Twas not their infirmity,
It was married chastity.

Truth may seem, but cannot be;
Beauty brag, but 'tis not she:
Truth and Beauty buried be.

To this urn let those repair
That are either true or fair;
For these dead birds sigh a prayer.

EDGAR ALLAN POE (1809–49)

THE RAVEN

Once upon a midnight dreary, while I pondered, weak and weary,
Over many a quaint and curious volume of forgotten lore —
While I nodded, nearly napping, suddenly there came a tapping,
As of some one gently rapping, rapping at my chamber door.
"'Tis some visiter," I muttered, "tapping at my chamber door —
                Only this and nothing more."

Ah, distinctly I remember it was in the bleak December;
And each separate dying ember wrought its ghost upon the floor.
Eagerly I wished the morrow; — vainly I had sought to borrow
From my books surcease of sorrow — sorrow for the lost Lenore —
For the rare and radiant maiden whom the angels name Lenore —
                Nameless *here* for evermore.

And the silken, sad, uncertain rustling of each purple curtain
Thrilled me — filled me with fantastic terrors never felt before;
So that now, to still the beating of my heart, I stood repeating
" 'Tis some visiter entreating entrance at my chamber door; —
                This it is and nothing more."

Presently my soul grew stronger; hesitating then no longer,
"Sir," said I, "or Madam, truly your forgiveness I implore;
But the fact is I was napping, and so gently you came rapping,
And so faintly you came tapping, tapping at my chamber door,
That I scarce was sure I heard you" — here I opened wide the door; —
                Darkness there and nothing more.

Deep into that darkness peering, long I stood there wondering, fearing,
Doubting, dreaming dreams no mortal ever dared to dream before;
But the silence was unbroken, and the stillness gave no token,
And the only word there spoken was the whispered word, "Lenore?"
This I whispered, and an echo murmured back the word, "Lenore!"
                Merely this and nothing more.

Back into the chamber turning, all my soul within me burning,
Soon again I heard a tapping somewhat louder than before.
"Surely," said I, "surely that is something at my window lattice;
Let me see, then, what thereat is, and this mystery explore—
Let my heart be still a moment and this mystery explore;—
                          'Tis the wind and nothing more!"

Open here I flung the shutter, when, with many a flirt and flutter,
In there stepped a stately Raven of the saintly days of yore;
Not the least obeisance made he; not a minute stopped or stayed he;
But, with mien of lord or lady, perched above my chamber door—
Perched upon a bust of Pallas just above my chamber door—
                          Perched, and sat, and nothing more.

Then this ebony bird beguiling my sad fancy into smiling,
By the grave and stern decorum of the countenance it wore,
"Though thy crest be shorn and shaven, thou," I said, "art sure no craven,
Ghastly grim and ancient Raven wandering from the Nightly shore—
Tell me what thy lordly name is on the Night's Plutonian shore!"
                          Quoth the Raven "Nevermore."

Much I marvelled this ungainly fowl to hear discourse so plainly,
Though its answer little meaning—little relevancy bore;
For we cannot help agreeing that no living human being
Ever yet was blessed with seeing bird above his chamber door—
Bird or beast upon the sculptured bust above his chamber door,
                          With such name as "Nevermore."

But the Raven, sitting lonely on the placid bust, spoke only
That one word, as if his soul in that one word he did outpour.
Nothing farther then he uttered—not a feather then he fluttered—
Till I scarcely more than muttered "Other friends have flown before—
On the morrow *he* will leave me, as my Hopes have flown before."
                          Then the bird said "Nevermore."

Startled at the stillness broken by reply so aptly spoken,
"Doubtless," said I, "what it utters is its only stock and store
Caught from some unhappy master whom unmerciful Disaster
Followed fast and followed faster till his songs one burden bore—
Till the dirges of his Hope that melancholy burden bore
                              Of 'Never – nevermore.' "

But the Raven still beguiling my sad fancy into smiling,
Straight I wheeled a cushioned seat in front of bird, and bust and door;
Then, upon the velvet sinking, I betook myself to linking
Fancy unto fancy, thinking what this ominous bird of yore—
What this grim, ungainly, ghastly, gaunt, and ominous bird of yore
                              Meant in croaking "Nevermore."

This I sat engaged in guessing, but no syllable expressing
To the fowl whose fiery eyes now burned into my bosom's core;
This and more I sat divining, with my head at ease reclining
On the cushion's velvet lining that the lamp-light gloated o'er,
But whose velvet-violet lining with the lamp-light gloating o'er,
                              She shall press, ah, nevermore!

Then, methought, the air grew denser, perfumed from an unseen censer
Swung by seraphim whose foot-falls tinkled on the tufted floor.
"Wretch," I cried, "thy God hath lent thee—by these angels he hath
    sent thee
Respite—respite and nepenthe from thy memories of Lenore;
Quaff, oh quaff this kind nepenthe and forget this lost Lenore!"
                              Quoth the Raven "Nevermore."

"Prophet!" said I, "thing of evil!—prophet still, if bird or devil!—
Whether Tempter sent, or whether tempest tossed thee here ashore,
Desolate yet all undaunted, on this desert land enchanted—
On this home by Horror haunted—tell me truly, I implore—
Is there – *is* there balm in Gilead?—tell me—tell me, I implore!"
                              Quoth the Raven "Nevermore."

"Prophet!" said I, "thing of evil!—prophet still, if bird or devil!
By that Heaven that bends above us—by that God we both adore—
Tell this soul with sorrow laden if, within the distant Aidenn,
It shall clasp a sainted maiden whom the angels name Lenore—
Clasp a rare and radiant maiden whom the angels name Lenore."
                                        Quoth the Raven "Nevermore."

"Be that word our sign of parting, bird or fiend!" I shrieked,
        upstarting—
"Get thee back into the tempest and the Night's Plutonian shore!
Leave no black plume as a token of that lie thy soul hath spoken!
Leave my loneliness unbroken!—quit the bust above my door!
Take thy beak from out my heart, and take thy form from off
        my door!"
                                        Quoth the Raven "Nevermore."

And the Raven, never flitting, still is sitting, *still* is sitting
On the pallid bust of Pallas just above my chamber door;
And his eyes have all the seeming of a demon's that is dreaming,
And the lamp-light o'er him streaming throws his shadow on the
        floor;
And my soul from out that shadow that lies floating on the floor
                                        Shall be lifted—nevermore!

ANON

COCK ROBIN

Who killed Cock Robin?
I, said the Sparrow,
With my bow and arrow,
I killed Cock Robin.

Who saw him die?
I, said the Fly,
With my little eye,
I saw him die.

Who caught his blood?
I, said the Fish,
With my little dish,
I caught his blood.

Who'll make his shroud?
I, said the Beetle,
With my thread and needle,
I'll make the shroud.

Who'll dig his grave?
I, said the Owl,
With my pick and shovel,
I'll dig his grave.

Who'll be the parson?
I, said the Rook,
With my little book,
I'll be the parson.

Who'll be the clerk?
I, said the Lark,
If it's not in the dark,
I'll be the clerk.

Who'll carry the link?
I, said the Linnet,
I'll fetch it in a minute,
I'll carry the link.

Who'll be chief mourner?
I, said the Dove,
I mourn for my love,
I'll be chief mourner.

Who'll carry the coffin?
I, said the Kite,
If it's not through the night,
I'll carry the coffin.

Who'll bear the pall?
We, said the Wren,
Both the cock and the hen,
We'll bear the pall.

Who'll sing a psalm?
I, said the Thrush,
As she sat on a bush,
I'll sing a psalm.

Who'll toll the bell?
I, said the Bull,
Because I can pull,
I'll toll the bell.

All the birds of the air
Fell a-sighing and a-sobbing,
When they heard the bell toll
For poor Cock Robin.

GEOFFREY CHAUCER (1342–1400)

from 'THE NUN'S PRIEST'S TALE' in THE CANTERBURY TALES

This Chanticleer stood high upon his toes,
He stretched his neck, his eyes began to close,
His beak to open; with his eyes shut tight
He then began to sing with all his might.
Sir Russel Fox leapt in to the attack,
Grabbing his gorge he flung him o'er his back
And off he bore him to the woods, the brute,
And for the moment there was no pursuit.
O Destiny that may not be evaded!
Alas that Chanticleer had so paraded!
Alas that he had flown down from the beams
O that his wife took no account of dreams!
And on a Friday too to risk their necks!
O Venus, goddess of the joys of sex,
Since Chanticleer thy mysteries professed
And in thy service always did his best,
And more for pleasure than to multiply
His kind, on thine own day, is he to die?

JOHN BETJEMAN (1906–84)

DIARY OF A CHURCH MOUSE
(Lines, written to order on a set subject, to be spoken on the wireless.)

Here among long-discarded cassocks,
Damp stools, and half-split open hassocks,
Here where the Vicar never looks
I nibble through old service books.
Lean and alone I spend my days
Behind this Church of England baize.
I share my dark forgotten room
With two oil-lamps and half a broom.
The cleaner never bothers me,
So here I eat my frugal tea.
My bread is sawdust mixed with straw;
My jam is polish for the floor.
  Christmas and Easter may be feasts
For congregations and for priests,
And so may Whitsun. All the same,
They do not fill my meagre frame.
For me the only feast at all
Is Autumn's Harvest Festival,
When I can satisfy my want
With ears of corn around the font.
I climb the eagle's brazen head
To burrow through a loaf of bread.
I scramble up the pulpit stair
And gnaw the marrows hanging there.
  It is enjoyable to taste
These items ere they go to waste,
But how annoying when one finds
That other mice with pagan minds
Come into church my food to share
Who have no proper business there.
Two field mice who have no desire
To be baptized, invade the choir.
A large and most unfriendly rat

Comes in to see what we are at.
He says he thinks there is no God
And yet he comes . . . it's rather odd.
This year he stole a sheaf of wheat
(It screened our special preacher's seat),
And prosperous mice from fields away
Come in to hear the organ play,
And under cover of its notes
Ate through the altar's sheaf of oats.
A Low Church mouse, who thinks that I
Am too papistical, and High,
Yet somehow doesn't think it wrong
To munch through Harvest Evensong,
While I, who starve the whole year through,
Must share my food with rodents who
Except at this time of the year
Not once inside the church appear.
　　Within the human world I know
Such goings-on could not be so,
For human beings only do
What their religion tells them to.
They read the Bible every day
And always, night and morning, pray,
And just like me, the good church mouse,
Worship each week in God's own house,
　　But all the same it's strange to me
How very full the church can be
With people I don't see at all
Except at Harvest Festival.

EDWARD LEAR (1812–88)

THE POBBLE WHO HAS NO TOES

The Pobble who has no toes
    Had once as many as we;
When they said, 'Some day you may lose them all;'—
He replied,—'Fish fiddle de-dee!'
And his Aunt Jobiska made him drink,
Lavender water tinged with pink,
For she said, 'The World in general knows
There's nothing so good for a Pobble's toes!'
The Pobble who has no toes,
    Swam across the Bristol Channel;
But before he set out he wrapped his nose
    In a piece of scarlet flannel.
For his Aunt Jobiska said, 'No harm
Can come to his toes if his nose is warm;
And it's perfectly known that a Pobble's toes
Are safe,—provided he minds his nose.'
The Pobble swam fast and well,
    And when boats or ships came near him
He tinkledy-binkledy-winkled a bell,
    So that all the world could hear him.
And all the Sailors and Admirals cried,
When they saw him nearing the further side,—
'He has gone to fish, for his Aunt Jobiska's
Runcible Cat with crimson whiskers!'
But before he touched the shore,
    The shore of the Bristol Channel,
A sea-green Porpoise carried away
    His wrapper of scarlet flannel.
And when he came to observe his feet,
Formerly garnished with toes so neat,
His face at once became forlorn
On perceiving that all his toes were gone!
And nobody ever knew
    From that dark day to the present,

Whoso had taken the Pobble's toes,
  In a manner so far from pleasant.
Whether the shrimps or crawfish gray,
Or crafty Mermaids stole them away—
Nobody knew; and nobody knows
How the Pobble was robbed of his twice five toes!
The Pobble who has no toes
  Was placed in a friendly Bark,
And they rowed him back, and carried him up,
  To his Aunt Jobiska's Park.
And she made him a feast at his earnest wish
Of eggs and buttercups fried with fish;—
And she said,—'It's a fact the whole world knows,
That Pobbles are happier without their toes.'

EDWARD LEAR (1812–88)

THE OWL AND THE PUSSY-CAT

1

The Owl and the Pussy-cat went to sea
   In a beautiful pea-green boat,
They took some honey, and plenty of money,
   Wrapped up in a five-pound note.
The Owl looked up to the stars above,
   And sang to a small guitar,
"O lovely Pussy! O Pussy, my love,
   What a beautiful Pussy you are,
         You are,
         You are!
   What a beautiful Pussy you are!"

2

Pussy said to the Owl, "You elegant fowl!
   How charmingly sweet you sing!
O let us be married! too long we have tarried:
   But what shall we do for a ring?"
They sailed away, for a year and a day,
   To the land where the Bong-tree grows
And there in a wood a Piggy-wig stood
   With a ring at the end of his nose,
         His nose,
         His nose,
   With a ring at the end of his nose.

3

"Dear Pig, are you willing to sell for one shilling
   Your ring?" Said the Piggy, "I will."
So they took it away, and were married next day
   By the Turkey who lives on the hill.
They dined on mince, and slices of quince,

Which they ate with a runcible spoon;
And hand in hand, on the edge of the sand,
They danced by the light of the moon,
The moon,
The moon,
They danced by the light of the moon.

'Not all that tempts your wandering eyes
And heedless hearts, is lawful prize;
 Nor all that glisters, gold.'

from 'Ode'

THOMAS GRAY (1716–71)

ODE
On the Death of a Favorite Cat, Drowned in a Tub of Goldfishes

'Twas on a lofty vase's side,
Where China's gayest art had dyed
   The azure flowers that blow;
Demurest of the tabby kind,
The pensive Selima, reclined,
   Gazed on the lake below.

Her conscious tail her joy declared;
The fair round face, the snowy beard,
   The velvet of her paws,
Her coat, that with the tortoise vies,
Her ears of jet, and emerald eyes,
   She saw; and purred applause.

Still had she gazed; but 'midst the tide
Two angel forms were seen to glide,
   The genii of the stream:
Their scaly armor's Tyrian hue
Through richest purple to the view
   Betrayed a golden gleam.

The hapless nymph with wonder saw:
A whisker first and then a claw,
   With many an ardent wish,
She stretched in vain to reach the prize.
What female heart can gold despise?
   What cat's averse to fish?

Presumptuous maid! with looks intent
Again she stretched, again she bent,
   Nor knew the gulf between.
(Malignant Fate sat by and smiled)
The slippery verge her feet beguiled,
   She tumbled headlong in.

Eight times emerging from the flood
She mewed to every watery god,
    Some speedy aid to send.
No dolphin came, no Nereid stirred;
Nor cruel Tom, nor Susan heard;
    A favorite has no friend!

From hence, ye beauties, undeceived,
Know, one false step is ne'er retrieved,
    And be with caution bold.
Not all that tempts your wandering eyes
And heedless hearts, is lawful prize;
    Nor all that glisters, gold.

CHRISTOPHER SMART (1722–71)

MY CAT, JEOFFREY

For I will consider my Cat Jeoffrey.

For he is the servant of the Living God, duly and daily serving him.

For at the First glance of the glory of God in the East he worships in his way.

For is this done by wreathing his body seven times round with elegant quickness.

For then he leaps up to catch the musk, which is the blessing of God upon his prayer.

For he rolls upon prank to work it in.

For having done duty and received blessing he begins to consider himself.

For this he performs in ten degrees.

For first he looks upon his fore-paws to see if they are clean.

For secondly he kicks up behind to clear away there.

For thirdly he works it upon stretch with the fore-paws extended.

For fourthly he sharpens his paws by wood.

For fifthly he washes himself.

For sixthly he rolls upon wash.

For Seventhly he fleas himself, that he may not be interrupted upon the beat.

For Eighthly he rubs himself against a post.

For Ninthly he looks up for his instructions.

For Tenthly he goes in quest of food.

For having consider'd God and himself he will consider his neighbour.

For if he meets another cat he will kiss her in kindness.

For when he takes his prey he plays with it to give it a chance.

For one mouse in seven escapes by his dallying.

For when his day's work is done his business more properly begins.

For he keeps the Lord's watch in the night against the adversary.

How he counteracts the powers of darkness by his electrical skin and glaring eyes.

For he counteracts the Devil, who is death, by brisking about the life.

For in his morning orisons he loves the sun and the sun loves him.

For he is of the tribe of Tiger.

For the Cherub Cat is a term of the Angel Tiger.

For he has the subtlety and hissing of a serpent, which in goodness he
   suppresses.

For he will not do destruction, if he is well fed, neither will he spit
   without provocation.

For he purrs in thankfulness, when God tells him he's a good Cat.

For he is an instrument for the children to learn benevolence upon.

For every house is incomplete without him and a blessing is lacking in
   the spirit.

For the Lord commanded Moses concerning the cats at the departure of
   the Children of Israel from Egypt.

For every family had one cat at least in the bag.

For the English Cats are the best in Europe.

For he is the cleanest in the use of his fore-paws of any quadrupede.

For the dexterity of his defence is an instance of the love of God to him
   exceedingly.

For he is the quickest to his mark of any creature.

For he is tenacious of his point.

For he is a mixture of gravity and waggery.

For he knows that God is his Saviour.

For there is nothing sweeter than his peace when at rest.

For there is nothing brisker than his life in motion.

For he is of the Lord's poor and so indeed is he called by benevolence
   perpetually—Poor Jeoffrey! poor Jeoffrey! the rat has bit thy throat.

For I bless the name of the Lord Jesus that Jeoffrey is better.

For the divine spirit comes about his body to sustain it in complete cat.

For his tongue is exceedingly pure so that it has in purity what it wants
   in music.

For he is docile and can learn certain things.

For he can set up with gravity which is patience upon approbation.

For he can fetch and carry, which is patience in employment.

For he can jump over a stick which is patience upon proof positive.

For he can spraggle upon waggle at the word of command.

For he can jump from an eminence into his master's bosom.

For he can catch the cork and toss it again.

For he is hated by the hypocrite and miser.
For the former is affraid of detection.
For the latter refuses the charge.
For he camels his back to bear the first notion of business.
For he is good to think on, if a man would express himself neatly.
For he made a great figure in Egypt for his signal services.
For he killed the Ichneumon-rat very pernicious by land.
For his ears are so acute that they sting again.
For from this proceeds the passing quickness of his attention.
For by stroking of him I have found out electricity.
For I perceived God's light upon him both wax and fire.
For the Electrical fire is the spiritual substance, which God sends from
    heaven to sustain the bodies both of man and beast.
For God has blessed him in the variety of his movements.
For, tho he cannot fly, he is an excellent clamberer.
For his motions upon the face of the earth are more than any other
    quadrupede.
For he can tread to all the measures upon the music.
For he can swim for life.
For he can creep.

T. S. ELIOT (1888–1965)

MACAVITY: THE MYSTERY CAT

Macavity's a Mystery Cat: he's called the Hidden Paw—
For he's the master criminal who can defy the Law.
He's the bafflement of Scotland Yard, the Flying Squad's despair:
For when they reach the scene of crime—*Macavity's not there*!

Macavity, Macavity, there's no one like Macavity.
He's broken every human law, he breaks the law of gravity.
His powers of levitation would make a fakir stare,
And when you reach the scene of crime—*Macavity's not there*!
You may seek him in the basement, you may look up in the air—
But I tell you once and once again, *Macavity's not there*!

Macavity's a ginger cat, he's very tall and thin;
You would know him if you saw him, for his eyes are sunken in.
His brow is deeply lined with thought, his head is highly domed;
His coat is dusty from neglect, his whiskers are uncombed.
He sways his head from side to side, with movements like a snake.
And when you think he's half asleep, he's always wide awake.

Macavity, Macavity, there's no one like Macavity,
For he's a fiend in feline shape, a monster of depravity.
You may meet him in a by-street, you may see him in the square—
But when a crime's discovered, then *Macavity's not there*!

He's outwardly respectable. (They say he cheats at cards.)
And his footprints are not found in any file of Scotland Yard's.
And when the larder's looted, or the jewel-case is rifled,
Or when the milk is missing, or another Peke's been stifled,
Or the greenhouse glass is broken, and the trellis past repair—
Ay, there's the wonder of the thing! *Macavity's not there*!

And when the Foreign Office find a Treaty's gone astray,
Or the Admiralty lose some plans and drawings by the way,
There may be a scrap of paper in the hall or on the stair—
But it's useless to investigate—*Macavity's not there*!
And when the loss has been disclosed, the Secret Service say:
'It *must* have been Macavity!'—but he's a mile away.
You'll be sure to find him resting, or a-licking of his thumbs,
Or engaged in doing complicated long division sums.

Macavity, Macavity, there's no one like Macavity,
There never was a Cat of such deceitfulness and suavity.
He always has an alibi, and one or two to spare:
At whatever time the deed took place—MACAVITY WASN'T THERE!
And they say that all the Cats whose wicked deeds are widely known
(I might mention Mungojerrie, I might mention Griddlebone)
Are nothing more than agents for the Cat who all the time
Just controls their operations: the Napoleon of Crime!

T. S. ELIOT (1888–1965)

THE SONG OF THE JELLICLES

Jellicle Cats come out tonight,
Jellicle Cats come one come all:
The Jellicle Moon is shining bright—
Jellicles come to the Jellicle Ball.

Jellicle Cats are black and white,
Jellicle Cats are rather small;
Jellicle Cats are merry and bright,
And pleasant to hear when they caterwaul.
Jellicle Cats have cheerful faces,
Jellicle Cats have bright black eyes;
They like to practise their airs and graces
And wait for the Jellicle Moon to rise.

Jellicle Cats develop slowly,
Jellicle Cats are not too big;
Jellicle Cats are roly-poly,
They know how to dance a gavotte and a jig.
Until the Jellicle Moon appears
They make their toilette and take their repose:
Jellicles wash behind their ears,
Jellicles dry between their toes.

Jellicle Cats are white and black,
Jellicle Cats are of moderate size;
Jellicles jump like a jumping-jack,
Jellicle Cats have moonlit eyes.
They're quiet enough in the morning hours,
They're quiet enough in the afternoon,
Reserving their terpsichorean powers
To dance by the light of the Jellicle Moon.

Jellicle Cats are black and white,
Jellicle Cats (as I said) are small;
If it happens to be a stormy night
They will practise a caper or two in the hall.
If it happens the sun is shining bright
You would say they had nothing to do at all:
They are resting and saving themselves to be right
For the Jellicle Moon and the Jellicle Ball.

ANON

THE KILKENNY CATS

There were once two cats of Kilkenny,
Each thought there was one cat too many;
So they fought and they fit,
And they scratched and they bit,
  Till, excepting their nails,
  And the tips of their tails,
Instead of two cats, there weren't any.

LOUIS MACNEICE (1907–63)

DOGS IN THE PARK

The precise yet furtive etiquette of dogs
Makes them ignore the whistle while they talk
In circles round each other, one-man bonds
Deferred in pauses of this man-made walk
To open vistas to a past of packs

That raven round the stuccoed terraces
And scavenge at the mouth of Stone Age caves;
What man proposes dog on his day disposes
In litter round both human and canine graves,
Then lifts his leg to wash the gravestones clean,

While simultaneously his eyes express
Apology and contempt; his master calls
And at the last and sidelong he returns,
Part heretic, part hack, and jumps and crawls
And fumbles to communicate and fails.

And then they leave the park, the leads are snapped
On to the spiky collars, the tails wag
For no known reason and the ears are pricked
To search through legendary copse and crag
For legendary creatures doomed to die
Even as they, the dogs, were doomed to live.

'Little Lamb, who made thee?
Dost thou know who made thee?'

from 'The Lamb'

ANON

THE NAMES OF THE HARE
from the Middle English (version by Seamus Heaney)

The man the hare has met
will never be the better of it
except he lay down on the land
what he carries in his hand—
be it staff or be it bow—
and bless him with his elbow
and come out with this litany
with devotion and sincerity
to speak the praises of the hare.
Then the man will better fare.

'The hare, call him scotart,
big-fellow, bouchart,
the O'Hare, the jumper,
the rascal, the racer.

Beat-the-pad, white-face,
funk-the-ditch, shit-ass.

The wimount, the messer,
the skidaddler, the nibbler,
the ill-met, the slabber.

The quick-scut, the dew-flirt,
the grass-biter, the goibert,
the home-late, the do-the-dirt.

The starer, the wood-cat,
the purblind, the furze cat,
the skulker, the bleary-eyed,
the wall-eyed, the glance-aside
and also the hedge-springer.

The stubble-stag, the long lugs,
the stook-deer, the frisky legs,
the wild one, the skipper,
the hug-the-ground, the lurker,
the race-the-wind, the skiver,
the shag-the-hare, the hedge-squatter,
the dew-hammer, the dew-hopper,
the sit-tight, the grass-bounder,
the jig-foot, the earth-sitter,
the light-foot, the fern-sitter,
the kail-stag, the herb-cropper.

The creep-along, the sitter-still,
the pintail, the ring-the-hill,
the sudden start,
the shake-the-heart,
the belly-white,
the lambs-in-flight.

The gobshite, the gum-sucker,
the scare-the-man, the faith-breaker,
the snuff-the-ground, the baldy skull,
(his chief name is scoundrel.)

The stag sprouting a suede horn,
the creature living in the corn,
the creature bearing all men's scorn,
the creature no one dares to name.'

When you have got all this said
then the hare's strength has been laid.
Then you might go faring forth—
east and west and south and north,
wherever you incline to go—
but only if you're skilful too.
And now, Sir Hare, good-day to you.
God guide you to a how-d'ye-do
with me: come to me dead
in either onion broth or bread.

ANON

THE FROG

What a wonderful bird the frog are—
When he sit, he stand almost;
When he hop, he fly almost.
He ain't got no sense hardly;
He ain't got no tail hardly either.
When he sit, he sit on what he ain't got—almost.

WILLIAM BLAKE (1757–1827)

THE LAMB

Little Lamb, who made thee?
　　Dost thou know who made thee?
Gave thee life & bid thee feed,
By the stream & o'er the mead;
Gave thee clothing of delight,
Softest clothing wooly bright;
Gave thee such a tender voice,
Making all the vales rejoice!
　　Little Lamb who made thee?
　　Dost thou know who made thee?

Little Lamb I'll tell thee,
　　Little Lamb I'll tell thee!
He is callèd by thy name,
For he calls himself a Lamb:
He is meek & he is mild,
He became a little child:
I a child & thou a lamb,
We are callèd by his name.
　　Little Lamb God bless thee.
　　Little Lamb God bless thee.

OGDEN NASH (1902–71)

THE PIG

The pig, if I am not mistaken,
Supplies us sausage, ham, and bacon.
Let others say his heart is big—
I call it stupid of the pig.

OGDEN NASH (1902–71)

THE COW

The cow is of the bovine ilk;
One end is moo, the other, milk.

NORMAN MACCAIG (1910–96)

FETCHING COWS

The black one, last as usual, swings her head
And coils a black tongue round a grass-tuft. I
Watch her soft weight come down, her split feet spread.

In front, the others swing and slouch; they roll
Their great Greek eyes and breathe out milky gusts
From muzzles black and shiny as wet coal.

The collie trots, bored, at my heels, then plops
Into the ditch. The sea makes a tired sound
That's always stopping though it never stops.

A haycart squats prickeared against the sky.
Hay breath and milk breath. Far out in the West
The wrecked sun founders though its colours fly.

The collie's bored. There's nothing to control . . .
The black cow is two native carriers
Bringing its belly home, slung from a pole.

THEODORE ROETHKE (1908–63)

THE SLOTH

In moving-slow he has no Peer.
You ask him something in his Ear,
He thinks about it for a Year;

And, then, before he says a Word
There, upside down (unlike a Bird),
He will assume that you have Heard —

A most Ex-as-per-at-ing Lug.
But should you call his manner Smug,
He'll sigh and give his Branch a Hug;

Then off again to Sleep he goes,
Still swaying gently by his Toes,
And you just *know* he knows he knows.

WILLIAM CARLOS WILLIAMS (1883–1963)

THE HORSE

The horse moves
independently
without reference
to his load

He has eyes
like a woman and
turns them
about, throws

back his ears
and is generally
conscious of
the world. Yet

he pulls when
he must and
pulls well, blowing
fog from

his nostrils
like fumes from
the twin
exhausts of a car.

LOUIS MACNEICE (1907–63)

CIRCUS CANTO IV: ELEPHANTS

Tonnage of instinctive
Wisdom in tinsel,
Trunks like questions
And legs like tree trunks

On each forehead
A buxom blonde
And round each leg
A jangle of bells,

Deep in each brain
A chart of tropic
Swamp and twilight
Of creepered curtains,

Shamble in shoddy
Finery forward
And make their salaams
To the tiers of people—

Dummies with a reflex
Muscle of laughter
When they see the mountains
Come to Mahomet . . .

Efficacy of engines,
Obstinacy of darkness.

ACKNOWLEDGEMENTS

— ◇ —

The publishers would like to acknowledge the following for permission to reproduce copyright material. Every effort has been made to trace copyright holders but in a few cases this has proved impossible. The publishers would be interested to hear from any copyright holders not here acknowledged.

3. Faber and Faber Ltd for 'Address to the Beasts' from *Collected Poems* by W.H. Auden.

6. Faber and Faber Ltd for 'The Horses' from *Collected Poems* by Edwin Muir.

8. J.M. Dent for 'The Ancients of the World' from *Collected Poems 1945–1990* by R.S. Thomas, published by J.M. Dent & Sons.

9. Faber and Faber Ltd for 'Elephants' from *Complete Poems* by Marianne Moore.

12, 156. Faber and Faber Ltd for 'The Hippopotamus' and 'The Song of the Jellicles' from *Collected Poems* by T.S. Eliot.

14. A.P. Watt Ltd on behalf of the Royal Literary Fund for 'The Donkey' from *Poems for All Purposes* (Pimlico, 1984) by G.K. Chesterton.

15. 'The Frog in the Swimming Pool' is from *Off-Season at the Edge of the World* by Debora Greger. Copyright 1994 by Debora Greger. Used with permission of the poet and the University of Illinois Press.

17, 100. 'Hares at Play' and 'The Badger' are from *John Clare: The Oxford Authors*, ed. Eric Robinson and Geoffrey Summerfield (Oxford University Press, 1984). Reproduced with permission of Curtis Brown Group Ltd, London, on behalf of Eric Robinson. Copyright © Eric Robinson 1984.

19. A.P. Watt Ltd on behalf of Michael B. Yeats for 'The Wild Swans at Coole' from *The Collected Poems of W.B. Yeats*.

20, 126. Faber and Faber Ltd for 'The Horses' and 'The Thought-Fox' from *The Hawk in the Rain* by Ted Hughes.

25. Faber and Faber Ltd for 'The Cormorant in Its Element' from *Collected Poems* by Amy Clampitt.

26, 28, 128, 170. 'Kingfisher', 'Solitary Crow', 'Toad' and 'Fetching Cows' are from *Collected Poems* by Norman MacCaig, published by Hogarth Press.

27, 48. 'Sandpiper' and 'The Fish' are from *The Complete Poems 1927–1979* by Elizabeth Bishop. Copyright © 1979, 1983 by Alice Helen Methfessel. Reprinted with the permission of Farrar, Straus and Giroux, LLC.

29, 168, 169. 'The Duck', 'The Pig' and 'The Cow' are from *I Wouldn't Have Missed It* by Ogden Nash, published by Andre Deutsch Ltd (1983).

34, 35. Faber and Faber Ltd for 'Considering the Snail' and 'Apartment Cats' from *Selected Poems* by Thom Gunn.

36, 113. The James MacGibbon Estate for 'The Galloping Cat' and 'The Singing Cat' by Stevie Smith.

38. Faber and Faber Ltd for 'Brock' from *Meeting the British* by Paul Muldoon.

44, 63, 71. Laurence Pollinger Ltd and the Estate of Frieda Lawrence Ravagli for 'Mosquito', 'Snake' and the extract from 'Eagle in New Mexico' from *The Complete Poems of D.H. Lawrence.*

47. 'The Trout' from *Collected Poems, 1995* by John Montague is reproduced by kind permission of the author and The Gallery Press, Loughcrew, Oldcastle, Co. Meath, Ireland.

55. Faber and Faber Ltd for 'The Tame Hare' from *Rock Face* by Norman Nicholson.

56. 'The Bear on the Delhi Road' is from *Collected Poems 1975* by Earle Birney. Used by permission, McClelland & Stewart, Ltd. *The Canadian Publishers.*

58, 124. Faber and Faber Ltd for 'The Arrival of the Bee Box' and 'Black Rook in Rainy Weather' from *Collected Poems* by Sylvia Plath.

60. 'A Narrow Fellow in the Grass' from *The Poems of Emily Dickinson*, ed. Thomas H. Johnson, is reprinted by permission of the publishers and the Trustees of Amherst College, Cambridge, Mass.: the Belknap Press of Harvard University Press. Copyright 1951, 1955, 1979 by the President and Fellows of Harvard College.

61. Oxford University Press for permission to reprint 'Snakes' from *The Striders: Poems* by A.K. Ramanujan (1966). © Oxford University Press 1966.

66, 87, 123. The Estate of Robert Frost for 'Come In', 'Design' and 'Dust of Snow' from *The Poetry of Robert Frost* edited by Edward Connery Lathem, published by Jonathan Cape.

70. A.P. Watt Ltd on behalf of The National Trust for Places of Historic Interest or Natural Beauty for 'The Hyaenas' from *Rudyard Kipling's Verse: Definitive Edition.*

74. 'The Vulture' is from *Complete Verse* by Hilaire Belloc, published by Random House UK Ltd. Reprinted by permission of the Peters Fraser and Dunlop Group Ltd on behalf of: The Estate of Hilaire Belloc. © Estate of Hilaire Belloc 1970.

75, 77, 98. Faber and Faber Ltd for 'Hawk Roosting', 'Thrushes' and 'An Otter' from *Lupercal* by Ted Hughes.

76. Sheil Land Associates Ltd for 'Owl' from *A Doomsday Book* by George MacBeth (Scorpion Press, 1965). © George MacBeth 1965.

79. Faber and Faber Ltd for the extract from *Beowulf*, version by Seamus Heaney.

84. 'The Pike' by Edmund Blunden (Copyright © Edmund Blunden 1919) is reproduced by permission of the Peters Fraser and Dunlop Group Ltd on behalf of the Estate of Mrs Claire Blunden.

86. 'The Killer Snails' is from *The Memory of War & Children in Exile* by

James Fenton, published by Penguin. Reprinted by permission of the Peters Fraser and Dunlop Group Ltd.

91, 171. Faber and Faber Ltd for 'The Meadow Mouse' and 'The Sloth' from *Collected Poems* by Theodore Roethke.

93. A.P. Watt Ltd on behalf of Michael B. Yeats for 'Lonely the Sea-Bird Lies at Her Rest' from *The Collected Plays of W.B. Yeats*.

94. John Murray (Publishers) Ltd for 'The Hawk' from *Selected Poems* by George Mackay Brown.

97. Carcanet Press for 'The Dead Crab' from *Selected Poems* (1998) by Andrew Young.

140. The extract from 'The Nun's Priest's Tale' is from Nevill Coghill's translation of *The Canterbury Tales* by Geoffrey Chaucer (Penguin Classics, 1977). Copyright 1951 by Nevill Coghill. Copyright © Nevill Coghill, 1958, 1960, 1975, 1977. Reproduced by permission of Penguin Books.

141. John Murray (Publishers) Ltd for 'Diary of a Church Mouse' from *Collected Poems* by John Betjeman.

154. Faber and Faber Ltd for 'Macavity: the Mystery Cat' from *Old Possum's Book of Practical Cats* by T.S. Eliot.

159, 173. David Higham Associates for 'Dogs in the Park' and 'Circus Canto IV: Elephants' from *Collected Poems* by Louis MacNeice, published by Faber and Faber.

163. Faber and Faber Ltd for 'The Names of the Hare' from *Opened Ground* by Seamus Heaney.

172. Carcanet Press for 'The Horse' from *Collected Poems* (1988) by William Carlos Williams.

INDEX OF POETS' NAMES

— ◇ —

INDEX OF FIRST LINES

— ◇ —